just Be LOVE

Unveiling Love, Light, Perfection & Freedom

Trenia Today

BOOK DESIGN & INTERIOR LAYOUT: JR Arthur of Pixel Munki
EDITOR: Chanette Sparks of IBJ Marketing
EDITOR: Jessica Wyche
EDITOR: Thomas Mburu

DEDICATION

First and foremost I would like to dedicate this book to my Creator and Father God. It has been a journey getting here to this point but I could have not done any of this without you. I next would like to dedicate this book to all the Cosmic Beings, Gods & Goddesses, Archangels and Archaii, Elohim's and last but not least The Ascended Masters of the Great White Brotherhood! Walking into this information has been life changing...but I always knew there was so much more to the Universe than what we all have been taught.

I thank you for choosing me to share this with the world and particularly the Christian Community. I promise I will share and speak in LOVE as all of you have.

I thank my daughter Jessica for always being there with me. She has walked with me throughout this whole book. I also dedicate this book to my youngest daughter Kyerra whom has aspired me very much. Much gratitude and love!

My heart is humble, grateful, and thankful. I am looking forward to teaching!

FORWARD

When Trenia Today connected with me about expressing my thoughts for this book, Just Be Love; I was excited, fearful, overwhelmed all at the same time. I had the wonderful opportunity to meet this savvy, educated, and beautiful woman, however, I wasn't sure what to expect. While reading, I began to relax and unwind, while tuning in to a world that many of us do not speak openly about.

FORGIVENESS. LOVE. KARMA. PEACE.

This book and the amazing title shares a refreshed approach to the imperfections of the world we live in and how we all should handle unforeseen circumstances that could affect us into adulthood. If you are someone who has ever struggled with religious beliefs or even if you are someone with an open mind to spirituality, this book is definitely for you!

As humans, we experience life in unpredictable ways which sometimes alert us to acknowledge what we are going through. In order to better our lives, we must become one with ourselves and take a leap into spirituality to clear our hearts of all jealousy, hatred and envy.

Trenia Today discovered her true purpose and passion in life many years ago while working diligently to support her two young daughters. She began a spiritual journey of entrepreneurship and wholeness while having a spiritual encounter with GOD.

The greatest benefits that can be mastered from this lesson filled book is to understand that we all have a gift in life, as well as a mission to fulfill to better our world.

Beyond the personal changes that Trenia Today endured throughout her life, she obtained valuable information and resources from the Ascended Masters that she believed would offer value to living sustainable lifestyles. With unlimited and everlasting love, we can all blossom positively for ourselves and for others.

In reading, you will find that life is more than what it appears to be and that we must encounter occasional highs and lows to reach future opportunities. When we have overcome things of challenge through understanding, knowledge, and meditation, we will then develop into productive human beings.

THIS BOOK IS SIMPLY REMARKABLE!

We are all different. Everyone in the world has a different story and will travel their own essential journey to peace, however, Trenia Today has narrowed down the key points and incentives that will help us adapt and step out on faithful platforms.

I enjoyed learning that our chain of events can be controlled by our reactions to what is going on around us.

Life is too short to live inside of a box. There is so much for the body, mind, and spirit to thrive from in our economy. Trenia Today gives her all and her teachings of love are inspirational and fulfilling.

AUTHOR'S NOTE

IT IS TRULY AN HONOR TO BE CHOSEN TO WRITE SUCH A BOOK. This book was written to inspire and motivate you. To help you find YOU and be a positive family member of your community. We have lost all sense of what the word "Love" means. Love has turned into lust, hatred, unforgiveness, selfishness, jealousy and the list goes on.

What if you could live in a world of perfect peace? What if you can create your own world of perfect peace? What if you can contribute to your community and the world to make it a better place?

Love is energy and negativity is energy. What you put out is what you get back. It is the Law of Attraction. The Universal Law applied is to send out Divine Love at all times.

SEND OUT DIVINE LOVE AT ALL TIMES. . .

Jesus told us that the greatest commandment is love. Sadly most of us can quote it, remember it but do not practice it. I have learnt that it is because they do not love themselves nor really like themselves, because they do not know themselves. I am writing this book in mind with the thousands of people I have personally counseled motivated and inspired as well as those who will be touched and consciousness expanded through the reading of this book.

Father God & Mother Divine (Goddess) created a Perfect world and we were created to be perfect. The world has blocked that from you and have caused many to fear and have their minds controlled.

" I AM WRITING THIS BOOK IN MIND WITH THE THOUSANDS OF PEOPLE I HAVE PERSONALLY COUNSELED MOTIVATED AND INSPIRED. . . "

It is time to come back to YOU and rediscover your "I AM Presence." Time to learn to take care of the earth, love one another, love the animals, love the nature and the elementals of this beautiful earth. It is time to pour out Divine Love at all times.

I always said that God created a beautiful world and He wanted us to see it. I always planned on seeing it and have started and cannot wait to continue the journey. That same journey is there for you. We were called to be FREE and not SLAVES. It is time for each of us to wake us consciously as that is the only way to experience "The Second Coming of Christ" and make the ascension this lifetime.

We have moved into a new age, a new era, a higher dimension. We are ONE and are entering into an age of miracles. Your "I AM Presence" will never leave you the great God of your being each day. The God I Am that I Am the beloved "I AM Presence." Most are waiting for a rapture event but the Second coming of Christ is the awakening of YOU. You awakening into your seven bodies to get to your "I Am Presence."

I am the way the truth and the light. I am the open door. I am the resurrection and the life. I am the love of God that is always victorious. I am LOVE. There is a strong energy moving through the universe now and it is called Love. It is sending a vibration of divine love that will change hate, distress, bitterness and unforgiveness, into peace, serenity, happiness and well-being. Will you accept YOU?

Have you ever felt that there was something MORE to what you have been taught and was told to just "follow" what you have been taught and not to question it? I have.

What if I told you that Jesus is still alive today? He is still working to this day with all the Cosmic Beings. What if I told you that Jesus was not the "Only Begotten Son" and that there were unascended beings who taught the same message which is "DIVINE LOVE?." I am sure that will rock your boat a little bit. But keep reading because GOD want your eyes opened.

We are in a new age. The age of the Aquarius. Many souls are going to be enlightened during this time. Many are going to gain ascension this lifetime. Are you ready to gain your ascension?

I am sure you are saying "What ascension," "Who are the Ascended Masters," What are Ascended Masters? Trust me... it was all very foreign to me as well. However, the more I studied ...it just made sense. Everything in me told me that this was the truth. I was chosen to open a door for you. To show you something different and the truth. To lead you to answers to questions you have been asking for a while. Keep reading this book. We have the answers for you and this is just the beginning or your new Spiritual Journey to your I Am Presence! After you read this book and to further your Spiritual Growth and really discover your I AM Presence passages have been extracted from the book "21 Essential Lessons" Volume 1. Compiled from the Teaching of the "Bridge to Freedom" by Werner Schroeder and published by The Ascended Master Teaching Foundation.

Lovingly & Peace,

Trenia Today

ACKNOWLEDGEMENTS

TO MY MOM AND DAD: Darrell and Jessica Gipson, thank you for all of your support. You've raised me to become the woman that I am "Today" and I owe you the world. You have been by my side every step of the way during my journey, and for that, I thank you from the bottom of my heart. I love you to the moon and back!

TO MY BROTHERS AND SISTER: Donald, Tesha, Tabarii and Danyell.; words cannot express enough of how grateful I am to have you as my siblings and friend. Thank you for loving me through everything and also being amongst my life in all ways possible. I will always love you!

ISIS STORM: Your love, support, encouragement, and sweet personality has helped me write this book. You have such a beautiful spirit and I love that so much about you. You are indeed a true friend and I will always value and love that about you.

"Lastly but not least. I would like to thank some very very dear people to my heart who have believed in me, my vision and given their time.

KYLA KNOX. . . Words cannot express the love and gratitude I feel towards you with our friendship. You have been the type of friend I only imagined. My first recording for "The Trenia Today Show" you were there...created my beautiful set and was supported in any way possible...genuine.That meant so much to me. You are the baddest Event Planner and Decorator I have ever met. I am looking forward to a beautiful, full of life, traveling, and a beyond lifetime friendship with you. Thank you My Love! I KNOW Success is written all over you. . .your heart is priceless!

LIZ CREWS. . . You are the type of friend that we roll together. I can talk about anything spiritual and positive under the sun. I knew when we met it was not just a business relationship... you are truly a lifetime friend. Thank you for all your love, support , and honesty!

Now it is time for me to support you in all your dreams... because you My Love have too much to offer to the world. Let the journey begin!

PHAEDRA TAYLOR. . . Our knowing each other has been brief to to this day of publishing. But one thing I do know is that your heart is pure and genuine...You are one of the most beautiful woman I have ever met and I will always love you... thank you for your support and I totally 1000% support you in your upcoming Cooking Show!!! Beautiful people like you... need to spread the love world wide...I love you sis!

TANISHA WALTON. . . My best friend of many years, you have always been my biggest cheerleader and believed in me and the vision with a pure heart. Thank you for always being my friend and for allowing me to be god mommy to Tommy and Timmy...my two loves. I love you all very much and am looking forward to growing old with you as my best friend. You are irreplaceable!

SHAVANNAH MOORE. . . My "Mini-me" thank you for being a sweetheart and always smiling when I see you. You are dear to me and I thank God our paths have crossed. I am looking forward to watch you blossom. Never stop or give up, you are right there. I love you little sis!

JR ARTHUR. . . You have been GOD SENT!!! You not only captured the vision and created my whole visual brand. . .you blessed me in so many ways! This is just the VERY BEGINNING for us! I am eternally grateful for your generosity and belief in me. I am truly ready for all of us to ride this journey together. I know that you have nothing but blessings and success written with your name on it. Keep blessing people and watch how WE will NEVER forget you!

CHANETTE SPARKS. . . My lovely, humble and bad PR and Writer. I trust you with my life! I have never been able to say that about anybody. Your love, support, endless hours of devotion to all of these projects have been mind blowing. But. . .what is most important is your belief in me and the dream. I believe in you whole heartedly and EVERY SINGLE last one of your dreams are coming to past, that is for sure! You bless people unselfishly and your heart is always pure. I have never met anyone like you ever! Girl. . .I love you always. . .let's change the world together in a positive way and Just Be Love!

KEITH CRAWLEY. . . Last but absolutely not least, I can never forget the man that did not meet me, but believed in me. You sowed into the whole Trenia Today Brand. You gave me hope and reassurance that there are still good loving people out there. Words can never describe my gratitude. . .so me and God just have to show you. You are my friend for life and I need you. Long conversations and being able to just be me. . .no judgement is priceless. Thank you for believing and being there in more ways than anyone can imagine. I will always LOVE YOU and your family for generations to come. Thank you from the bottom of my heart and soul. . .you are a definite BLESSING!!!

TABLE
OF CONTENTS

DIVINE
LIVING

CHAPTER 1

"Where there is love there is life".
- Mahatma Gandhi -

The word love has been misused to such an extent, that every step of the way we question its meaning. We are living in a world of violent state. Hatred and greed is amongst many people. Your minds have been programmed with the things you watch on TV, listen to on the radio and watch on the internet.

All of these things are teaching violence, hate, jealousy, wrath, revenge and a "Me, Myself and I" attitude world. Nobody seems to want to help each other anymore. Do you even know your neighbors? What are their names? What do they do for a living? Have you bar-b-cued with each other, celebrated holidays together? We have lost the since of a community and the real meaning of love.

I remember growing up as a child everybody was "auntie" or "uncle" and respected them in your neighborhoods. We were able to play outside all day, we could even leave from the front of our house and go around the neighborhood. Life was fun then and kids played with kids outside. Back then, people seemed to be filled with love, laughter, and happiness.

What happened? Where has the love gone? Countries are constantly fighting over each other and most of it has to do with Religion. Religion is not love and these days it has been turned into a form of mind control, hatred, cultish, separateness and constant discord.

GOD IS PEACE!

GOD is PEACE. Those who have the Holy Spirit feel that God is in you. With this, we need to be spreading the kind of LOVE you feel that God will do. God is not a mean God, and God is not a judgmental God. As a matter of fact, there is no judgment at all. Everyone creates their own Karma with poor decisions and the lack of love.

We were created in the image of God and we have been here

for millions of years. Yes! YOU are an old soul and have been living on the birth and rebirth wheel. There is no death. Most fear this truth, as they think there is no life beyond this life and you either go to Heaven or Hell. That is simply not true. I am here to share with you that you have re-embodied many, many, many of times.

If you expand your mind and begin to search for the truth inside of YOU, you will find yourself. God has sent his people on a mission to restore and heal others. It is time for you to contribute your part to the oneness and start spreading and being LOVE.

It is time for your consciousness to open up. It is time for you to remember who YOU really are. Life is beautiful and it was meant for us all to enjoy and learn from it. Can you imagine if everybody start to work on themselves personally? What if people began to love unconditionally? What if the masses of the people sent out divine love all the time? Imagine how the energy vibrations on the earth would change. You are the director and you have the power to direct and co-create your life with God.

How do I pour divine love all the time? You have the power to program the flame of divine love by pouring out love all the time. While you go on with your daily activities, it can be as simple as putting on some beautiful music and letting it play throughout the day. Even when you leave your home, leave the music on lightly to fill your home with energy while you're gone.

For any soul of life there must be a pouring of divine love before the "I AM" began to flow. We all have an "I AM" presence.

*The Use of the Word "I AM"
(Extracted from 21 Essential Lessons Vol. 1)

The word "I AM" is the CREATIVE WORD OF THE UNIVERSE, used by all God-Beings EVERYWHERE for that purpose - not just on earth! When a call is made using the word *"I AM,"* this is a signal to intelligent life to create. *LIFE, WHICH IS INTELLIGENT, WILL OBEY YOU.* The call compels the answer! It always has!

Every creation that lives in our world, constructively or otherwise, is the result of the obedience of the life to your command, somewhere upon life's way, Turn to the constructive, positive, conscious use of the powers of the creative words, *"I AM"* and *PROVE TO YOURSELF* that intelligent life will manifest *ACCORDING TO YOUR DECREE.* There is no greater teacher than one's own experiences!

"I AM" is God's very own, most sacred and holy name – so said Moses long ago. Jesus learned the power of the creative word "I AM" and used it, enjoying the buoyant, uplifting feeling of the constructive use of any statement preceded by the words *"I AM."* For example, he used the statement, *"I AM* the resurrection and the life."

When you have said for centuries, "I am helpless, I am sick, I am distressed," you have built into this etheric garment, into that which the world calls the sub-conscious, certain deep grooves of energy. It is a consciousness which has accepted that which you have decreed for yourself for millions of years. You have done the same thing with your emotional body and your mental body through the misuse of life.

Now is the opportunity for the chelas of Great White Brotherhood to teach mankind that when using the creative words *"I AM,"* they should always be followed by a positive and constructive statement.

As there is no limit to the powers of the God-protection that can be called forth, and no limit to the transmuting power of the Cosmic Christ Love, *YOU HAVE EVERYTHING AT HAND* by which to draw forth, protect and sustain your God-endeavors!

When you become really advanced in your spiritual growth and development, you become the master of any situation. Then in one word you can say to the flood, *"STOP!"* You can say to the great earthquakes, *"CEASE!"* You can say to volcanic eruptions, *"BE STILL,"* and it will be done!

UNIVERSAL
FORCES

CHAPTER 2

"You've gotta dance like there's nobody watching, Love like you'll never be hurt, Sing like there's nobody listening, And live like it's heaven on earth."
- William W. Purkey -

LOVE IS. . .

Love is pure, true, crystallize, unconditional and seeking perfection. When you love in the simplest manner, it is to give pleasure to someone and thinking about their greatest good. Love has no boundaries or limits, and is blind to reason. Love is for everybody. It is open-minded for people to love everybody with a pure heart. Love loves their enemies and is universal. It sees no color, creed, religion, gender, nationality, sex etc. Love is God and comes from God. Love is pure in its rarest form.

PURE LOVE. . .

Pure love is just love with no motives or selfish reason for loving one another. There is a great difference between love and lust. Love wants what is best for the other, while lust want what is best for you only.

Pure love does not expect anything and does not demand. It is gracious, natural and freeing. Pure love brings you closer to yourself and your inner truth. It also maintains the highest attitude and vision for every person, animal, nature and elementals. Pure love is divine, constant and selfless.

Pure love is free from fear and resides in a state of freedom. Pure love's joy is the joy of giving. It is God in manifestation and is the strongest magnetic energy force in the universe. Ask and invite pure love into your life and heart. Let it transform, clean and energize you to another dimension beyond your wildest imagination. Pure love is free and cost nothing...just open your heart and begin to love everyone as one.

REAL LOVE. . .

Real love is not affected by situations around us and it tends to assume a stable state. Whether you offer praises or criticize and insult, it neither increases nor decreases. Real love knows no hostility and it does not puff up just because someone thinks highly of it. Through the eyes of this kind of love, the world has no blemishes or errors. The purity that comes with real love makes the human element of our God more tangible and palatable.

TRUE LOVE. . .

The external world does not know the meaning of love, neither can it comprehend the attributes of true love. In fact, what the world calls love is just a construct whose contents are attraction and infatuation. Love in its true humility resides near and within the person who has a grasp of self and its entire faculty; the majesty, glory and splendor.

True love is God, for He is the embodiment of that blameless, pure and perfect love. Love brings both physical and mental liberation. It is the path whose end is liberty of the human spirit. Even in a state of confusion, despair and discouragement, pure love is the panacea that heals all.

God is love and God is pure, He dwells in situations where there is honesty and sincerity of heart. God is only in places where there is faith and purity. If you look for Him in any other places where these things lack, and where there is no love, it will be hard to hear Him.

*"So never consider love as negative - it is always a positive aspect, but its expression may be in dynamic confidence, faith and protection. It may be illumination and understanding, in wonderful tolerance, in the spirit of the ascetic. It may be in the concentration of your energies upon something which will be of benefit to the whole universe. It may be in ministering in your hospitals or asylums to men and women in distress, in the using of the power of invocation as best you know how,

like the chemist in the laboratory, putting one and the other activity together until you have the divine alchemy of the Violet Fire. There is no greater love in the universe than that expressed by a man or woman who gets that perfect alchemy and the science that is behind it, and can transmute through example - at least to the student body – the science of the Violet Fire of Purification."

"You, beloved students, must cultivate the capacity to love and understand your fellowman. "That to which you give your life grows, multiples, develops and matures, whether it is a garden plot, a farm crop, or whether it is a friendship – human or divine. The pouring forth of the gratitude of your love and life multiplies and make things grow.

"Oh, the happiness that your bodies you will feel, and the lightness that you will experience, as you drop the appearances of age, distress and discomfort. As you learn to relax within that Pink Flame of Gratitude and Thanksgiving to life, the softness will erase the lines from your face and love will replace the hard look in the eyes. All these blessings come from the use of that Flame of Thanksgiving, of Gratitude and Adoration.

BEING CLOTHED WITH LOVE

The surest way to embody love, it to cast away the fault-finding spirit and see the world as it is; the beautiful virgin world, flawless as it is, populated with innocent beings that know neither evil nor wrong.

Looking through the lens of illusion, people are categorized as either good or bad. But really no one is bad after all! If anything God made us all good. Our attachment to real love is the primary reason why we see people as being good and our detachment from the core of pure love makes us see the errors and iniquities in others. The true spirit of unadulterated love is awakened the moment we change our perspective towards the world and instead of seeing the convolutions and the entanglements, we see it as being faultless.

The separatist mentality is what brings selfishness and jealousy. We only love what belongs to us and what we call our own everything else is 'theirs'. As long as this chasm that separates your dominion and that of the other person exists,

---

> " LISTEN CAREFULLY TO YOUR
> HEART, THERE ARE ALWAYS
> ANSWERS THERE. "

---

we shall continue to cling to what we recognize as ours and be detached from what belongs to them. Having such a hardliner position cannot make you an embodiment of true love.

Self is the true reflection of the love that can lift the burdens away and embrace you with such loving kindness that is greater than life. Love sprouts and spreads its tendrils when you take the initiative to earnestly ask for forgiveness. You have to put yourself at fault for having allowed yourself to see the corruption and evil in others. By taking this approach, you are cleansing yourself and gearing up to become an embodiment of love. It is only then will you have an opportunity to taste and see the authenticity of true love.

HOW TO BE A
TRUE IMAGE OF LOVE

One fundamental truth with pure love is that it tends to increase as the differences between us decrease; and inverse proportionality. The only thing that we need to develop and become is the image of this love with interpersonal differences. It is the surest way.

To become a personification of love, you have to deliberately break the glass walls that separate you and others to further embrace the spirit of oneness and selflessness. Individualism is like cancer that eats away the cells of pure love. In addition, it leaves behind a chronic disease of hatred and selfishness.

Loves becomes tangible when you take a bold step and plant, 'I' where there is 'You,' meaning that you will have to change the old perception of others and instead perceive self in all people. This will in turn erode the individual differences by bringing unity, purpose and strength.

The tendons that connect the big family under the sun will pull together around true love, which is the central pillar. It is then that the world will realize true love, peace and bring sorrows to a conclusive end.

LOVE IS NON-JUDGMENTAL

One night I went out on date with a man I met online. We met, laughed, talked and actually had a really good time. In the middle of the date he looked at me and said, "Trenia I really misjudged you. I looked at your pictures, your profession, how you appeared to carry yourself and I passed judgment on you". He said, "I am not going to tell you my thoughts, but just know you are nothing what I imagined you to be."

He went on to genuinely express how he thought I was really cool and down to earth. I loved his honesty and started laughing a bit and told him that he judged the book by its cover. Never judge a book by its cover, it may turn out to be the best book you have ever read. It turned out to be a very good evening once we moved past him passing judgment on who and what he thought my character was.

The point is to not judge people. Get to know a person before deciding how you feel towards them. Also be yourself! If people pass judgment on you it does not matter. That is something that they have to overcome personally. The ones who matter won't mind and the ones who mind don't matter.

You need to accept yourself the way you are as well as appreciating others for who they are. The basic fact of life has it that any struggle to change your real self may not yield much fruit but instead may leave a trail of frustrations and loss. Our differences consume us for a reason and we need to accept them in a gracious and loving manner.

" NO HUMAN RACE IS SUPERIOR; NO RELIGIOUS FAITH IS INFERIOR. ALL COLLECTIVE JUDGMENTS ARE WRONG. ONLY RACISTS MAKE THEM "
- Elie Wiesel -

By learning how to lend a helping hand, you will earn the respect of your family, your peers and all the other people around you. Enforce the habit of performing acts of kindness towards others and top these up with good deeds. In doing so, you will know what it means to live in the full energy of love and people will love and respect you for this.

When we look at others, we essentially see our own reflections in them. Every moment you point a finger or accuse someone else of faults, you tend to bring out your personality more than theirs. It is your own projections and prejudices that you are exposing by judging others.

WHEN ARE
WE ENTITLED
TO JUDGE OTHERS?

The question about when we should judge seems to resurface every now and then. Is there a time when we are justified in judging others? Do you ever look at yourself and access your ways before pointing a finger in judgment? You could be culpable of the same offence may be varying in magnitude or context.

Judging has an advantage to some degree has in the sense that self-improvement would be difficult to realize if others did not point out issues that are in our dark spots. Without realizing our flaws and weaknesses through the corrections of others, we would ultimately discover them the hard way. From my observation, we are not entitled to point fingers and judge others but we do it as a reflex action. It just happens unconsciously!

The reason we cannot truly judge others is that our carnal knowledge cannot allow us to know another entity outside our SELF confines so well. We do not have the capacity to judge what we do not fully understand. The human brain functions much like that of a computer, it uses judgment as a comparative measurement of value. It is through judgment that we get an opportunity to admire people. Judgment is a process that is wired in our systems and we often use it to distinguish between good and bad company.

The best approach to judgment is by keeping it to ourselves and recognizing that our limited knowledge does not give us such a wide berth to use in judging others. We should also bear in mind that new information could come in at any time that could have the potential of reversing earlier judgments.

Whether you call it gentle love or tough love, the fact remains that you have been loved. The easiest way to stop the reflex action of judging others is by removing the word judge and replacing it with support. I do not judge anyone because I have enough problems to myself. I have people that I do support. I talk to them as a friend and let them know that I have their best interest at heart. I tell them of what I feel is the best for them and what I believe will be disastrous if they pursue. Instead of forcing them to be my favor and adopt my way, I simply give them the options available that they can follow.

" WHEN YOU JUDGE ANOTHER, YOU DO NOT DEFINE THEM, YOU DEFINE YOURSELF "
- Wayne Dyer -

Our perception of others is the basis of our judgment. This is a truism that I have experienced in my own life and the many years I have spent counseling other people. We all come from different set ups, different backgrounds and environment. Unless we walk in others shoes, we may not exactly realize things the way they perceive them. Judging others without having the facts in our finger tips is actually playing a role that only God can.

My approach is not to judge others but rather provide them with a way that will make their life more meaningful. If I feel that I cannot help a situation or a person, I will not front any suggestion in fact I prefer to keep mum. I personally find people very receptive to hearing another person's opinion or suggestion when they are ready to change. We may not be in the best position to tell why others are doing things the way they do them. They could have gone through issues that we may not understand or alternatively, they could be deriving some benefits from doing things that way. This gives us more reason for not judging them. We can see and even point out a shortcoming in a manner that it will not amount to judgment.

In as much as we think we are a know-it-all, the truth is we are not. Having been in a situation similar to what another person is going through does not give us the mandate to judge them. Situations and circumstances change and our reaction too could have changed with time. Instead of judging, it could be more helpful if we offer an alternative way of handling a precipitating issue. You also need to bear in mind that just by your comments or opinions, the other person is bound to change. It depends with how they receive it and whether to change or not is their own volition.

CELEBRATE
AUTHORITY

CHAPTER 3

"People who make the choice to study, work hard or do whatever they endeavor is to give it the max on themselves to reach to the top level. And you have the people who get envy and jealous, yet are not willing to put that work in, and they want to get the same praise."
- Evander Holyfield -

LOVE IS NOT ENVIOUS OR JEALOUS

I have always been the type of person that celebrated other people's happiness and success. I always truly am happy and excited for them, whether I know them personally or not. Joy and happiness in the world creates a ton of positive energy. I am a natural born positive person, and ever since I can remember, I have always seen the best in people.

" GREED, ENVY, SLOTH, PRIDE AND GLUTTONY: THESE ARE NOT VICES ANYMORE. NO, THESE ARE MARKETING TOOLS. LUST IS OUR WAY OF LIFE. ENVY IS JUST A NUDGE TOWARDS ANOTHER SALE. EVEN IN OUR RELATIONSHIPS WE CONSUME EACH OTHER, EACH OF US LOOKING FOR WHAT WE CAN GET OUT OF THE OTHER. OUR APPETITES ARE OFTEN SATISFIED AT THE EXPENSE OF THOSE AROUND US. IN A DOG-EAT-DOG WORLD WE LOSE PART OF OUR HUMANITY. "

- Jon Foreman -

What I could never understand was why was people envied me or appeared jealous of me. I was always one to celebrate milestones with others, but often, didn't receive celebration in return. I have had "friends" who have had more money than I did, fancier cars, jobs, houses and husbands. It didn't make sense to me at the time because I was a single and working mother, raising two daughters on my own. I was living on Section 8, unmarried, decent car, and was in no relationship to cause for jealousy.

It took many years and many of friends and acquaintances before I realized they were jealous and envious of my confidence. My belief in myself, my fearless attitude, and my positive view on the world. It was not the material things that made all these people envious or jealous of me...it was simply me. I viewed the world at all times with a positive outlook. I never use negative words or excuse phrases such as "But, What If, I can't etc." Those words did not and still do not exist in my vocabulary.

" JUST ASK FOR THE LIFE OF YOUR DREAMS AND YOU WILL HAVE JUST THAT. "

So although I was a single mother raising kids and working hard on my jobs, people were jealous. That blew my mind totally because I would look at them with such admiration and happiness towards their lives. Some were envious and some were simply jealous. I had to find out what was the difference between the two because they are both similar in nature.

What I found is, "The main difference between envy and jealousy is that envy is an emotion related to coveting what someone else has, while jealousy is the emotion related to fear that something you have will be taken away by someone else."

COMPARISON CHART

ENVY	JEALOUSY
DEFINITION	
Envy means "to bear a grudge toward someone due to coveting what that person has or enjoys. "THE LONGING FOR SOMETHING SOMEONE ELSE HAS WITHOUT ANY ILL WILL INTENDED TOWARD THAT PERSON."	Jealous means "apprehensive or vengeful out of fear of being replaced by someone else." It can also mean "watchful" "anxiously suspicious," "zealous," or "expecting complete devotion." The last is normally applied to God.
EXAMPLE	
I envy her possessions or situation.	I am jealous that you like her over me.
EASY WAY TO REMEMBER	
Envy is the emotion when you want a possession someone else has.	Jealousy is the emotion when you fear you may be replaced in the affection of someone you love or desire.

Envy is a condition that sets in when we do not have a certain attribute that another person has. Jealousy on the other hand occurs when something we possess is threatened by an external party.

Envy involves two people while jealousy involves three. Envy is a knee-jerk reaction due to lack of something. Jealously comes out of a threat of losing that which we already have to someone else.

Even though the difference between jealousy and envy seems to be straightforward, people usually mistake the two. So where is the confusion?

One of the causes of confusion is semantic ambiguity relating to the word jealousy. Whenever you ask people to describe for you a situation where they felt jealous, there is a very high likelihood that they will narrate a situation where they felt envious. This has led many to believe that jealousy and envy are similar even though they are miles apart.

This means that when someone says that they are feeling jealous, you need to listen carefully lest it be a case of envy. Analyze the context and if possible seek for clarification by engaging the individual further.

Another problem associated with jealousy and envy is the fact that they move together. For instance, the rivalry to your

---

" ENVY IS IGNORANCE. "
- Ralph Waldo Emerson -

---

partner's affections that causes jealousy could also share some characteristics that could make you envious. This brings in some sought of complication.

Therefore feeling jealous could also mean that you are envious at the same time.

Jealousy and envy evoke different emotions. Envy carries with it an aura of inferiority while jealousy bears a sense of betrayal and outrage.

DEALING WITH ENVY

Envy is an emotion that can be hidden under a smile so that people may not easily realize it. This however makes it exhausting on the inside. If you are envious of everyone who is around you and you feel that there is nothing good, then the results can be depressing.

As opposed to the harmful effects of envy that are very conspicuous, the benefits may not be as visible. Some of the negative effects of envy include:

- *Distress and discontent.*
- *It enslaves us in our own contexts and denies us freedom.*
- *It often leads to bitterness and resentment.*
- *It provokes us to do the unthinkable.*
- *It drives us down the route of depression.*

Despite these negative connotations, our lives are always full of emotions resulting from jealously and envy. It is like a battle that rages against our hearts and souls. We are increasingly becoming envious of everything including other people's bank accounts, relationships, appearances and talents. Even though envy and jealousy do not contribute to our emotional growth, we still retain them anyway.

Time has come for you to break loose from chains of jealousy and envy. Every one of us desires a good life that is free from these two elements. But how do you overcome jealousy and envy?

You need to question yourself the hard way:

- *What impact does jealousy and envy have on you? Do they work for you?*
- *Do you consider yourself to be fun to live with? Do you sit and think how your loved ones feel when you are dissatisfied with your own life?*
- *What is it that you are lacking? Don't you have a house, a car or money? How do you quantify enough in your life? Do you look at material possession or there are other factors that you consider?*

- *Do you feel that you are at your rock bottom? If you got an assurance today maybe from your spouse, would you feel rejuvenated and refreshed?*

- *What is it that didn't occur in your life that you strongly feel that it should have? How do you measure success in your own terms?*

- *Do you at times feel sorry for yourself for things that are beyond your control? Do you really know what you want in life?*

- *Have you ever interrogated your skills, gifts and abilities to create a satisfying life? What is the amount of time you spend lamenting on things that you don't have?*

- *Have you ever considered that you can control how your mind thinks and your actions that can change the imbalance that you are feeling?*

A STEPWISE APPROACH TO OVERCOMING ENVY

You need to first recognize that you are the first beneficiary and that you have the power to control envy.

Deconstruction of envious feelings. To begin with you need to demand more of yourself. You have to stop thinking about what other people have and instead focus on the things that you have and be thankful for them. Look at your gifts and talents that God has given to you, the people that you have in your life, the many opportunities that are lying ahead of you and count every single one of them. Engage in thinking about these things each and every day and you will realize that with time this focus will far outweigh the time that you spend worrying and thinking about others.

Your problems could be more of a perception than a reality. Is it real that you have problems? Assess your health, look at your children and the issues that you face on a daily basis, and be attentive to all that is around you because nature in a way communicates to those who are attentive. Do not miss on the moments that God taps you just to get your attention. This attentiveness will give you control of your life and nothing will get you off guard.

Just the same way you thought yourself into, you need to think your way out. Because you decided to dwell in your thoughts, you ended up feeling envious. It is a personal choice that made you get into this situation and it will take a new choice for you to get out. There is no magic around it, what you need is a change of your thoughts, your value system and the beliefs that you embrace. Get into a new thought pattern that will challenge you.

You need a paradigm shift in your focus so that you concentrate on the goodness side of your life. One of the major reasons as to why we envy is the fact that we have taken our gifting and blessings for granted. We need to count them and take stock one by one. We should understand that we are talented, gifted and loved. The life you live is unique and it cannot be lived by anyone else except you. There are lots of reasons to be grateful for it.

You need to always remind yourself that no one is self-sufficient. It is our deficiencies that make us need one another. This means that when you compare your life with that of other people, you will always find a gap. Life is not even either, there will always be people who have more than you have and therefore better than you. You should appreciate that every one of us goes through the same problems, have weaknesses, trials just like anyone else. After all, this is what makes us human.

Keep away from people who attach value to the wrong things. If you spend time with people who like comparing what is latest in the fashion scene and everything else that is trending, you are going to gradually develop a desire that will be insatiable. On the other hand, if you spend your time with people who always talk about their cars, salaries or extravagant vacations, you are likely to fall into the deep pit of personal belongings comparison. Life is however more than all these things; there are greater things to pursue that will give you nobility.

Always spend time with people who are grateful in life. Gratitude just like any virtue is highly contagious. You can pick an inspirational book or find people who are contented in life and try to spend quality time with them. Come to think of it, they are everywhere; online or you can find them in person. The more you invest your time with such people, the more you inherit their spirit of gratitude and soon you will start becoming an attraction to others.

" YOU HAVE THE POWER AND STRENGTH TO MAKE IT THROUGH THE MOST CHALLENGING TIMES OF YOUR LIFE AND IF YOU STAY POSITIVE; YOU WILL SUCCEED IN THE MOST BEAUTIFUL WAYS POSSIBLE. "

Take time to understand the philosophy of marketers. Know that at the bottom of it all, they are into advertising and therefore responsible for fanning the flame. They capitalize on jealousy and envy to push their products our way. Their greatest point of sale is achieved by stirring a desire to possess what the other person has hence driving us into a spending spree. Be on the lookout for their tactics, recognize that they are just marketers and refuse to be enslaved by their propositions.

Learn to celebrate other people success. When others make a fortune, rejoice with them. When they receive something that you don't have but you desire, be happy for them. Stop looking at them as a threat and competition. Joy can never be depleted, it is an infinite resource. The major hurdle that you have to jump in order to overcome envy is learning to celebrate in the happiness of others.

Practice generosity. It will not be easy at the beginning but you need to force yourself and make it an essential habit and part of your lifestyle. Give your finances and time, your abilities, talents and skills. Engage in voluntary schemes in your community, support projects that enhance social justice and get involved in the affairs of the society. The more time you spend and the energy you expend with those who are less fortunate, the more you will feel satisfied and contended. This will effectively get rid of the allure of the other person's life and possessions.

Envy has enslaved us for such a long time. The moment however has come for you to break loose and free from the tentacles of envy and lead a more fulfilling life.

Below are three assignments that will help you to gain around perspective of the world in just a week:

- *For a period of one week, write down 100 blessings you have experienced in your life. Do it on a daily basis and never repeat them.*
- *Every week, locate a member of your family either through phone or in person and let them know how much you appreciate them and the blessings they are in your life.*
- *In the same week, volunteer at least once for around 8 hours with the homeless, just sharing with them whatever there is and write down your experiences.*

OVERCOMING JEALOUSY

To overcome jealousy, you need to change your behavioral and emotional set up. It begins with knowing yourself and becoming aware of who you are. Self-awareness will help in discovering that many of the projected stories that occupy your mind are just but a mere fallacy. This will give you clarity of thoughts and will prevent you from reacting to scenarios that do not exist. Anger and jealousy are products of a deep seated belief within your mind of things that are not true. By changing your belief system, you automatically change your imaginations and ultimately your destructive emotional reactions. Even if the situation at hand justifies a reaction, jealousy and anger are not the ways to go about it.

Never try to change jealousy or anger once you are at the centre of an emotional storm. Doing so can be likened to seizing the control on a car that is already skidding on ice. You first of all need to steer clear of the emotive situation before you can make a sober approach. This effectively means that you need to take control of the triggers of jealousy before they form into a ball of emotions.

If you want to permanently eliminate jealousy and anger emotions within a relationship, you need to change your co-beliefs of insecurity and alter your mental projections of the whereabouts of your partner.

HOW TO HANDLE JEALOUSY REACTION

- *You need to recover your personal power that will enable you take control of the situation while at the other end refraining from reactive behaviors.*

- *Change your focus and step back from what is going on in your mind. This will give you space and time to avoid an angry or jealous reaction and instead engage in something else.*

- *Identify and isolate the central beliefs that are responsible for firing up your emotional reactions.*

- *Create an awareness within you that will negate the beliefs in your mind.*

- *Cultivate a self-control virtue over your emotions and attention so that you can selectively choose the kind of stories that occupy your mind.*

Jealousy is a dynamic concept that is created by a number of components. This means that any solution to jealousy needs to address each of the components comprehensively. Some of these components include emotions, will power, perspectives, perceptions and beliefs. The moment you miss out on one of these components, you will end up leaving an open trap door where destructive emotions can enter your mental complex.

Through a simple set of exercises, you can successfully withdraw from the story in your mind so as to get an opportunity to refrain from any emotive reaction. You need to have a desire deep down within you to change your emotions and behaviors. With the willingness to learn and embrace the teachings, you can do it.

TRIGGERS OF JEALOUSY CONSTITUTE THE SET OF BELIEFS THAT FORM A SENSE OF INSECURITY

Low self-esteem is based on beliefs that we have which create a mental image of who we think we are. In order to eliminate this, we just need to change the belief system and the false image of self. Many people have thought of this process as complex and difficult but the fact is that they have not invested much in terms of the skills needed to make this happen. Once you Master the necessary skills, you will realize that it takes a little effort and you achieve a complete change of your belief system. The ultimate pathway is to stop believing the image and story in your mind. Remember, it takes more convincing and effort to believe while unbelieving requires less if any effort.

SELF-JUDGEMENT CAN AGGRAVATE INSECURITY FEELINGS

It may not be sufficient to know in our minds that we are indeed creating an emotion. This information alone will make the Inner Judge to criticize and abuse us for what we are undertaking. The Inner Judge is likely to use this information to send us on a downward emotional spiral which will further intensify our insecurity. If you feel strongly that you need to make a long lasting change, you need to develop the necessary skills that will help you in dissolving the false self-images and unfounded beliefs. This will in turn help you in gaining control of your mind and what it projects.

" LISTEN CAREFULLY TO YOUR HEART, THERE ARE ALWAYS ANSWERS THERE. "

One of the key steps for behavior change requires that we see the process through which we create an emotion of jealousy or anger from the beliefs, images or assumptions resident in our minds. This step gives us an opportunity to take responsibility for our emotions and empower us to change them.

In case you are in a relationship with a partner who is jealous and they require that you change your behavior so that you can prevent their jealousy, they are not taking charge. Instead, they are creating an atmosphere of powerlessness so that they can use it as a bait to control your behavior.

THE MECHANISM THROUGH WHICH THE MIND CREATES ANGER AND JEALOUSY EMOTIONS

In the discussion below, I have highlighted the dynamics of the concept of jealousy and anger. This will be essential in filling some knowledge gaps with reference to the way in which your mind alters information and uses it for self-judgment which mostly results into insecurity and low self-esteem. This may help to create awareness but it is not sufficient either. For real and effective changes, you will need to adopt a different skills set. Just by knowing how your mind creates emotional reactions does not give you the power to enable you to change them.

For my description and illustration, I will make use of a woman whom I will refer to as the jealous party. In my scenario, the woman initiates the process by becoming jealous of her partner. Deep in her mind, she feels that she is not good enough and therefore insecure. This creates a Hidden False Image within her. With this mental projection, she starts to look down on herself and rejects her self-worth. This snowballs into feelings of unworthiness, unhappiness, fear and insecurity.

DEALING WITH INSECURITY

As a way of tackling the insecurity and the other emotions associated with the Hidden False Image, the woman goes ahead to create a Positive False Image through focusing on her positive qualities and attributes. The Positive False Image characterizes how she wants to be treated, seen and handled. This focus on the positive side of her and the resulting image completely eliminates any feelings of self-rejection, unworthiness and insecurity.

She gradually accepts herself and attracts love and happiness. One thing you need to realize is that she has not changed. The only thing that has happened is that she has had a change of slide where the Hidden False Image slide has been swapped with the Positive False Image slide.

The mental set up of the woman associates the Positive False Image with the qualities that men look for while the Hidden False Image is assumed to contain attributes that are not desirable at all and hence the cause of low self-esteem. Depending on the image she dwells on, she will strengthen the beliefs associated with it. It is the wolf that you feed that will become stronger.

What changes the emotion of the woman is her action to love and acceptance. It is neither the image nor the attention of the man that will change her emotional set up. The latter are only but triggers that activate the belief system of the woman; not change factors.

The mind of the woman is somehow dependent on the assumptions derived from the man. If she thinks that the man makes her happy, then she will indeed be happy. What she does not realize is that the man is only a trigger and he does not determine her happiness. In fact, she has full control of her own happiness and she can have it with or without the man.

CONTROLLING BEHAVIOR

The woman thrives from the false belief and assumption that the attention of the man is on her. This makes her happy and she feels appreciated. The moment she imagines that the attention has shifted to another person, she starts becoming fearful and the avalanche of negative attributes is triggered. The fear does not originate from the fact that she is about to lose the man as her belief may falsely suggest but rather the fear emanates from her inability to control the emotional pain that she has created in her mind through the Hidden False Image.

The diversion of his attention activates the Hidden False Image and the beliefs associated with it. This is when she feels worthless, insecure and unhappy about herself.

She goes ahead to engage in activities that will give her control over the man's attention. She does this so that her Positive False Image can be activated. This in turn works on her positive belief system and she once again sees herself as being worthy. In all this, what she does not understand is that the expression of love and acceptance is totally within her control and not in her partner.

USING ANGER AND PUNISHMENT AS BEHAVIORAL CONTROLS

One of the techniques that we learn from childhood is that by using anger we can control the emotions of others. For instance, whenever we were disciplined as children, we had a tendency of becoming angry at the person that did it. Harsh words that were seasoned with anger were also used as means of getting our attention. This mechanism was ingrained in our system and we did not unlearn it as we grew up meaning that it is part and parcel of our lives even today.

A jealous woman would tend to use anger so that they can take captive of the man's attention. In this set up, anger can also work as a punishment which results infliction of pain on the part of the man. By expressing anger through punishment, the woman aims at changing the behavior of the man so as to avoid any future emotional punishment.

One thing to observe in this scenario is that the use of anger is triggered by the false belief and not necessarily by the intellect of the woman. There could be other preferred choices to handle the situation but based on her emotional reactions powered by the Hidden False Image, she decides to be angry.

ANGER IS ENTRENCHED IN US FROM CHILDHOOD.

THE OUTCOME OF CONTROLLING ANGER

The use of anger is entrenched in us from childhood. In the adulthood context however, the results of the anger can be the exact opposite. Adults have more choices when it comes to punishment of anger. They can decide to walk away and leave their partners alone. What this will do on occasion is cause an activation of the woman's Hidden False Image beliefs. This in turn takes her through a cycle of depression, defeat, low self-esteem and unhappiness. This can be emotionally painful.

THE ANALYSIS
OF THE AFTERMATH

What follows after an incident of anger and jealousy is an opportunity to look back and do an analysis of the events. On the part of the woman, this can generate a considerable amount of emotional pain as her self-judgment rates her the lowest.

What exactly happens is that after such an event, the Inner Judge takes over. Because the Inner Judge rules from the point of the Positive False Image, it will condemn the woman and insist that she did not live to her expectations. Based on this ruling, the woman will consider herself a failure and good for nothing. Remember, these rulings will continue as long as the incident plays in the mind of the woman.

THE INNER JUDGE IS NEVER FAIR

The ruling of the Inner Judge concerning the anger incident puts the woman in the position of the Hidden False Image description. When the woman accepts this judgment and believes in it, she then transforms her feelings to those of guilt, shame and unworthiness. The ruling also cements the perspective and the character of the Hidden False Image which is negative.

The Inner Judge is never fair and in fact, he is likened to a hanging judge. The Inner Judge does not take cognizant of the fact that there is a belief system, there are false images and distorted point of views. At this point, the woman is at the mercy of what goes in her mind, a majority of which she has not been trained for. With training however, she can learn how to take control of her emotional state.

THE SPEED OF
THE CHAIN EVENTS

One thing you need to appreciate is that the emotions and the self-images inside the woman are flipped so fast. This makes her to some extent lose balance and awareness of what goes in her mind and the role of the belief system. The denial stage that sets in almost immediately also leads her mind into ignoring the Hidden False Image which results into emotional pain. Because of the speed and the number of elements in the reaction, there is likelihood that some elements may be missed. Missing out on these elements affects the conclusion and sobriety of judgment and ultimately dampens our efforts to change.

WHY EFFORTS TO
CHANGE BEHAVIOR
MAY BE FUTILE

The central problem that the woman faces is that she analyses the events from the perspective of the inner judge. This is the same judge who condemns and adds an element of self-rejection. The judgment reinforces the belief that the woman underperformed according to the standard of perfection. This perspective then reinforces the Hidden False Image and its associated beliefs. The result of all these is a futile attempt at behavioral change.

According to the reasoning of the woman, if she can only shift the paradigm of the unworthiness and project a Positive False Image then she can become confident, kind, strong and loving. These attributes will in turn make her attractive to the man. What she does not see is that the Positive False Image is a construct of her own imagination.

PROBLEMS ASSOCIATED WITH THIS APPROACH

The feelings of not being good enough can easily undermine the Positive False Image. Even though the Positive False Image may project a perfect you, this will only be temporal. The bedrock which is the Hidden False Image will be like a sipping aquifer bringing to the surface feeling of unworthiness continuously until it is dealt with.

Even if the woman succeeds in installing a Positive False Image, there will always be a coating of the Hidden False Image that casts a shadow of doubt on her ability to excel in everything she does. With these two belief systems in place, a feeling of inferiority will be hanging over giving her conflicting perspectives concerning herself. Despite the fact that she may be praised for the successes that she attains, deep within her the Hidden False Image will be reminding her that she is still the unworthy person she has always been. As long as the woman continues to associate herself and her identity with one or more of the images in her mind, the concept of Emotional Integrity will be elusive and difficult to attain.

The woman is always on guard so as to control her emotions. This feeling and state of being "on guard" is occasioned by fear that at any point in time she may lose control and her emotion will spill over. This state will eventually wear her down and in the long term, it will replace her emotions making her look unauthentic as far as love and happiness is concerned. A Positive False Image and the beliefs that come with it can help you in diminishing your emotive reactions but this has a limit. Remember that the Positive False Image is not the real you but rather a slide that helps you to cover temporarily your reactions. As long as the Hidden False Image and its associated beliefs still sit at the core of your behavioral system, you are bound to have outbursts of rage and jealousy which can be destructive because they come at a time when you are least prepared.

BEHAVIOR IS DRIVEN BY FALSE BELIEFS AND EMOTIONS

Anger and jealousy as a behavior used to control another person does not make much sense. The more we exude this behavior, the more we become unappealing to the other person and as a result they withdraw from us. Despite this, the woman will look at herself intellectually, see the vanity in her behavior but still stick onto it. Why is this, the case?

> ## ANGER AND JEALOUSY AS A BEHAVIOR USED TO CONTROL ANOTHER PERSON DOES NOT MAKE MUCH SENSE.

The reason behind it is that her behavior is not powered by any logic; intellectual knowing or thinking rather it is driven by False Images, Beliefs, Emotions and distorted Point of

View. This explains why logic cannot change such a behavior. In order to succeed in changing such a behavior, we must use another approach that does not incorporate intellect and logic. Any attempt at using logic will put us in the same bench with the inner judge who uses the same elements to create rulings that reinforce false beliefs.

THE RIGHT PATH

To succeed in changing beliefs, you have to Master your own point of view, and dissolve any false beliefs that are in your mind. By learning how to shift your perspective, you will be able to effectively move yourself out of an emotion and belief system to a new stand point. At this new platform, you will then develop an awareness that will help you see the faulty logic and the erroneous beliefs that controlled your behavior. Armed with this awareness, you can then be able to refrain from emotionally destructive behaviors. When you successfully eliminate the false beliefs, the triggers to your emotions are also eliminated. This will ultimately result into dissolution of your fears. Changing of behavior starts with a study of the problem and then taking action and solving it.

Jealousy develops in a relationship even in situations where the partners are very happy with one another. Out of the fear of loss especially of a treasured partner, the other part may become overly possessive. The more precious the partner becomes, the more threatened they feel losing them and this leads to overprotection.

Elimination of jealousy is not a quick and a one-off process. It is a trait that is embedded in character that affects emotions and the frame of mind. This means that getting rid of it will require a lot of work, patience, persistence and self-reflection.

The encouraging thing however is that the rewards of overcoming jealousy are uncountable. You will be free for your entire life and any relationship you get into will be meaningful and successful.

PROVEN STEPS OF DEALING WITH AND OVERCOMING JEALOUSY

Overcoming jealousy can be easy or difficult depending on the approach you take. To deal effectively with this problem, you first of all need to accept that you are a victim. Most of the people who struggle with jealousy may not be aware that they are dealing with denial. When you recognize that you are truly suffering, then you will be able to put in the necessary measures to ensure that the problem is solved. Following a successful identification and acceptance of the problem, the following easy to follow steps will ensure that the problem is eliminated completely and no trace of its manifestation is left.

- *You have to develop trust and know that whatever your partner does is to the best for the two of you. This should also come with the realization that your actions of espionage will not deter them from doing whatever they have purposed to do. Unless you have reasons to believe, kindly stop it!*

- *You need to keep in mind that your attractiveness and general appeal is what makes your partner stick with you. There are so many options available but because you have a quality that is rare and desirable, they will keep on being around you. Therefore, stop mounting pressure because being jealous cannot stop them from going away.*

- *Whatever efforts you expend on keeping your partner may not have a positive impact on your relationship. If anything, they will cause undue pressure and you can be sure, no one enjoys that. Instead, let the bird fly away, if it is really yours, it will come back. Focus on self-development and forget for a while that you are part of a relationship. It helps to be a little selfish at times.*

" LIFE IS ONE BIG ROAD WITH LOTS OF SIGNS. SO WHEN YOU RIDING THROUGH THE RUTS, DON'T COMPLICATE YOUR MIND. FLEE FROM HATE, MISCHIEF AND JEALOUSY. DON'T BURY YOUR THOUGHTS, PUT YOUR VISION TO REALITY. WAKE UP AND LIVE! "

- Bob Marley -

- *Spend time in honing your career and lifetime ambitions. You can invest in learning a new language, take a class in a new field of your choice and just keep yourself occupied. This will make you engaged and give you a break from the worries and troubles that are associated with forever thinking that you are in a relationship. Furthermore, life means so much than just revolving around your partner in assessing their faithfulness. In doing this, you will attain a much healthier state of mind and your jealousy stunts will slowly fade away.*

- *Jealousy conceals your attractive qualities. This means that the moment you overcome it, the powerful you will emerge. Your confidence, common sense and creativity will take the centre stage making you wise and attractive to your partner. This is by far one of the easiest ways to demonstrate your great qualities. You just need to rise above jealously.*

- *Enjoy while it lasts. Even though the expiry date of relationship is not in black and white, one day it might just as well come into an end. What this means is that you need to be cautious but at the same time open to possibilities and options. Enjoy every bit while the relationship is still up and running. The reason behind its ending may be beyond the control of the two of you. Therefore, be positive always. As you fight jealousy, one of the things that you will realize is that a fresh breath of freedom will stream in and the pain of jealousy will be lifted away. Insecurity will be replaced with trust and together with your partner you will enjoy a stronger, better and happier relationship.*

SPEAKING
LIFE

CHAPTER 4

"True forgiveness is when you can say, "Thank you for that experience."
- Oprah Winfrey -

LOVE FORGIVES

Forgiveness is something most of us find very hard to do. How can you forgive someone who has wronged you in such a terrible manner? I personally have experienced some traumas and drama in my life.

I am going to share a few chain of events with you from my life, which I have found helped me become the women that I am today.

When I was 9 years old, I had a favorite cousin that I used to love to play with as a kid and she had an older brother. Their parents, also my aunt and uncle, were my favorites as well. One day while playing at my cousin's house, she and her brother were outside smoking weed. I had never seen them smoke weed before, nor did I know very much about it.

" THE WEAK CAN NEVER FORGIVE. FORGIVENESS IS THE ATTRIBUTE OF THE STRONG. "
- Mahatma Gandhi -

They asked me if I want to try it and being that I was only 9, I was very reluctant. My cousin's older brother pretty much put the joint to my mouth and told me to puff, hold and exhale, and I did. I was so young, that I didn't even realize what was about to follow beyond that moment of negative influence. I had unintentionally placed myself in a vulnerable situation, encountering something that no child should ever have to endure...molestation.

My cousin's brother began to touch me inappropriately shortly after teaching me to smoke weed. He began to blackmail me, telling me that if I didn't let him rub his penis around on me, he would tell my dad that I was smoking weed. Fearful of getting in any trouble, I let him continue to touch me sexually. It was disgusting and I didn't like it at all. My favorite cousin knew what was happening. She never spoke of it to me, however, I assume she knew more than she shared, as she was also the lookout person for their parents. I was never molested when my aunt and uncle were home, and because he was older, he was much older and not there all the time. It was when he was there and the parents were gone that it happened.

This happened repeatedly for approximately 2 years. Yes, I experienced being molested by my older male cousin until I was 11 years old. I was never forced to go to their home. They were my family and I still loved them. I also still loved my big cousin, even though he wasn't making good decisions.

Every time I said no and that I didn't want to do it, he would threaten that he would tell my dad. After my cousin molesting me for two years and me witnessing him touch others, I suddenly had enough. On the final occasion, I firmly denied him the opportunity to touch me and told him to go tell my dad that I was smoking weed. I told him I was going to tell everyone how he taught me how to smoke weed and how he'd been touching me since I was nine years old.

It immediately stopped. He never said anything and neither did I. My other cousin and I never discussed it either, even as I write this book 33 years later. As I look back, that was really the beginning of me truly taking charge of my life and what I would allow others to do or not do to me.

I was going to control my destiny.

I went on with my life to end up pregnant at 14, a mother by 15, and pregnant again during my senior year in high school. I was 18 when I graduated high school with two daughters, 3 weeks and 3 years old.

I hadn't spoken to my cousin who had taken advantage of me sexually in quite some time at this point, however; I do believe that what he did to me caused me to lead a life of promiscuity later on in life. While I did know that he had gone to jail from family gossip, we had not spoken at all until I received a phone call from him shortly after having my daughter. I was 18 years old.

He congratulated me on the birth of my second daughter and also for graduating. Then he said something to me that changed my life, he asked for my forgiveness for what he had done to me as a little girl.

Who forgives someone who violated them in such a way? I was defiled and stripped away my innocence! I knew what a penis look liked erect way before I should have and had seen a penis of basically a grown man.

" THE TRUTH IS, UNLESS YOU LET GO, UNLESS YOU FORGIVE YOURSELF, UNLESS YOU FORGIVE THE SITUATION, UNLESS YOU REALIZE THAT THE SITUATION IS OVER, YOU CANNOT MOVE FORWARD. "
- Steve Maraboli -

I had all these feelings go through me and it flooded a ton of emotions that I had suppressed for such a long time. As I thought more about it in those few seconds, it seemed liked eternity for me to answer him. The words slowly crept out of my mouth. "I forgive you". To my surprise, not only did I say it, I actually felt it. I decided I was not going to be a victim anymore. I was not going to live the rest of my life hating and living in bitterness. I also decided that "God" forgives us so why can't I forgive.

I was truly released that day! It was also a very special moment in my life where I realized I could control my destiny and that I was the captain of my own ship! I have been sailing freely ever since.

Years later, and after my molester's apology, life continued to take its course. I have never been fond of envy, nor gossip; so when placed in situations where it was used towards me, I did not accept it. Forgiveness is something that can take time, due to the need to heal and understand for many. I found that holding on to grudges would never get me anywhere in life, so to move past them, I had to forgive.

On another night far after, I was hanging out in the neighborhood with friends and family. A young lady decided to hit me due to some conflict, busting a 750ml bottle of Seagram's Gin over my head. I did not feel the impact because it happened so fast, I just knew that something hit me. I remember wearing all white that evening and I started to see something dark dropping on my clothes. I put my hand up to my head only to realize that there was an extremely large hump on the left side of my face.

I put my hand on it and turned around to look at my assailant, while she looked at me and said, "That's is for calling me a bitch". Needless to say, I lost my mind. I was going crazy over the fact that she literally had me drenched in blood. I had to be thrown in the car by family because I was bleeding profusely and trying to get to this girl who was running away, after hitting me upside my head.

I waited throughout the night and went to the emergency room the next day. I was steaming with anger from the incident, so I did not go after it happened that night. The doctors were shocked that I was still alive. She hit me right in my temple in a deadly spot. I had to get over 20 stitches down the left side of my eye and face.

I had double black eyes for about 2 weeks and a scar that was keloid up on the side of my face. We eventually went to court about it and almost go into another fight in the courtroom. She was detained that time.

Years had passed and I hadn't seen her since we were last in court. A good 10 years had gone by since that night. One day while getting a manicure and pedicure, I noticed that a girl just kept staring at me. I was about 5 times my normal size at the time, but apparently she recognized me.

" FORGIVENESS IS NOT AN OCCASIONAL ACT, IT IS A CONSTANT ATTITUDE. "
- Martin Luther King Jr. -

She finished her services and left the nail salon. However, about 3 minutes later she returned and walked right up to me and said, "Trenia, I am sorry for what I did to you. Can you please forgive me?" I immediately recognized her at that moment and I called her name. She acknowledged that it was her and I told her, "Baby, I forgave you a long time ago" and gave her a big hug.

She was shocked and in tears. She began to tell me that the incident changed her life as she went away to college and obtained her degree. She also shared that she had not had any peace in her life since that night. Her actions had left her feeling tormented by it and she needed it released off of her. She told me that she tried to leave the salon, but couldn't with getting my forgiveness.

I truly had forgiven her, as I was a minister at that time and had been for a while. It was easy for me to hug her and let her cry on my shoulders. I wish her peace and happiness to this day.

I can recall another time in my life that was tragic for me. I was raped and beaten in my apartment by two neighborhood "friends". They actually were going to kill me, but I managed to escape by locking them inside of my house. The lock was made in a weird fashion in my building, so the two had to jump from a two story window to escape.

I could not believe that I was just raped and beat the way I was. A friendly gay couple opened their home up to me at about 5am in the morning and allowed me to use their phone after the rape.

I remember sitting in the hospital having pictures snapped of me and some rape kits done. I also remember the piece of yellow condom that was pulled out of me by the doctor. I was not in my right mind for a long time after that, but about one month after the rape one of the guys was killed. My family and I attended his funeral, and I remember having so much hate inside of me at that moment in my life. His family was aware of what had happened to me and of course everyone looked at me quite crazy for even attending his funeral. I went because in my mind, I felt like justice had been served. I wanted to make sure that my rapist was really dead.

All the emotions, feelings, memories, words and thoughts of that night came flooding back in as I looked at my rapist lie in the casket. A young 19 year old gone. Karma became real to me that day.

I never looked at the world, men or "friends" again since the night of the rape.

However, there was still the other guy out there who participated in the rape as well. He went off of the radar for a long time, but we crossed paths again many years later. It was about 8 to 10 years later and I was now a minister. We were at a funeral for my brother-in-law, which was his friend. My family confirmed that he was present and I remember encountering so many different feelings. Prior to interacting, he kept staring at me and finally came up to me and said, "Do I know you"? I remember this wailing of emotions, anger, hatred, and everything you can possible imagine. I looked my rapist in his face and said "Yes, you know me...you raped me!" He looked at me and said, "That is you!"

He looked me in my eye and told me that he was a different person then. He shared that he did not know why they did what they did to me, and that he was under the assumption that it was cool. I was so angry and I blurted out, "By beating me!!!"

" FORGIVENESS HAS NOTHING TO DO WITH ABSOLVING A CRIMINAL OF HIS CRIME. IT HAS EVERYTHING TO DO WITH RELIEVING ONESELF OF THE BURDEN OF BEING A VICTIM–LETTING GO OF THE PAIN AND TRANSFORMING ONESELF FROM VICTIM TO SURVIVOR. "

- C.R. Strahan -

He apologized and had tears in his eyes. He asked me to forgive him. He handed me his cell phone and told me that I could call the police right then and there with his phone, and also that he would not run. I was stunned! But I believed him and felt his sincerity.

I forgave him and told him I forgave him. I did not take his cell phone. I did not call the police. I did have this flood of emotional release that overcame me and I felt FREE!

I did forgive my rapist and I let it go. It no longer hindered me. It no longer ruled me. It no longer sat idle in the back of my mind. I was finally free and at peace all because I forgave.

It does occur at times that your past and what you did or did not do may haunt you. It could be that you wronged someone or there is a decision you made that you regret over. Forgiveness is something that you do not do for others but yourself. Forgiveness is not an approval that what happened was right or justifiable but rather a permission that you grant yourself to move on with life.

Forgiveness is a deliberate choice that you have to make. It is not coercion or a chance event.

Do not surrender your inner power by reliving what happened. It is understandable that you cannot reverse the course of events that already passed but you have the capacity to control everything that happens now and in future. Continuous suffering gives away your power to the person who caused the suffering.

Do not harbor ill and negative feelings. Anger is just an outward expression of a hurting, fearful, guilty and grief stricken soul. Pain may not disappear completely but forgiveness has the power to deflate the emotional balloon giving you an opportunity to release the anger within you and bring the people in your life even closer.

Recovery may not have a definite timeline but it happens to all who choose to let go. People are different and making peace could be difficult and a lengthy process for some while to others it happens fast and spontaneously. Either way, there is an effort that a person has to make consciously each and every day in the path to forgiveness. Forgiveness brings to rest any elements of anger, hatred, bitterness and resentment. You cannot alter the events that took place earlier in your life but the power to decide how you respond to them, squarely lies within you. In case you did not receive support at the time you really needed it, use the time you have to give yourself that support.

It is important that you dialogue within yourself. What is it that someone could have told you long ago that was and still is so hurting? Write everything down without censoring even a single bit. Analyze what you are saying to yourself in an effort to establish truth and fairness. If you feel that you are being unfair to yourself, start generating new ways of reasoning. Horrible and hurtful words can live beyond their expiry date in your life if you let them.

Think about the things that can give you emotional closure. It could be that you need an apology or something else. Try and find your Minimal Effective Response-the action that you can easily do to resolve your painful experiences.

Practice sharing your experience with other people. When you extract a lesson from what happened to you, you will succeed in putting the experience in the right perspective. That is not all; you will put your entire emotional make up in check. It is possible for people to thrive and go through suffering simultaneously.

Without true forgiveness, peace cannot be attained. The legendary Dr. Martin Luther King Jr. once said, *"Forgiveness is not an occasional act; it is a permanent attitude."* Children learn lots of things from their parents and this also applies to forgiveness. When they see the parents forgiving one another, they will also replicate that act.

Forgiveness allows us to enjoy freedom within ourselves. The more we cling onto resentment and anger, the more we relinquish this freedom. When we withhold love and instead choose hatred, we waste huge amounts of energy. The perfect remedy is to let go of our acrimonious feelings through forgiveness.

FOUR STEPS TO FORGIVENESS AND RELINQUISHMENT OF ANGER

According to Dr. Fredrick Luskin, an authority in anger management and emotional healing, the following steps have been proven to be effective and powerful in the management of anger and pursuit of forgiveness.

1. *Close your eyes, and for about 20 seconds, picture the person who hurt or angered you. Let all your grievances come up. Notice what happens in your body -- acceleration of heart-beat, shallow breathing, tension, etc.*

2. *Now let go of this image and take some slow, deep abdominal breaths. Focus on your abdomen, and imagine the breath going down into it as you inhale. Expand your abdomen on each inhalation, and deflate your abdomen as you exhale. Take about five breaths and keep your focus on your abdomen. If your mind goes back to the person who hurt you or to anything else, bring the focus back to the rhythm of your breath and the movement of your abdominal muscles as you inhale and exhale.*

3. *Bring into your mind an image of someone you love very much, or a place of peace and beauty. Allow yourself to be flooded with the positive feelings this image elicits. Now bring those feelings down to the area around your heart. Allow the good feelings to penetrate your heart and soothe you.*

4. *Lastly, keep breathing the good feelings into your heart. Now take a look again at the person you are angry at. Let the good feelings protect you. The purpose of doing this step is to break the pattern of stress reactions that normally occur in your mind and body when you think of the person who hurt you. When you surround your heart with positive energy, the power the person has had over you begins to dissipate.*

Resentment is a habit that you build over time. Just like any other habit, it takes 21 days to completely change and be freed from its tentacles. This means that when you practice these four steps every time a person angers you for a period of 21 days, you will literally change your entire physical and mental reactions. This will ensure that you are safe from their power to hurt because your entire system will have been reprogrammed. This is the path to true freedom.

Contrary to popular belief that there is no forgiveness without reconciliation, it is possible to forgive unconditionally. It is understandable that the conventional means to forgiveness is through reconciliation, clearing of the emotive air and understanding one another. However, this is at times literally impossible. Picture this- the person who has wronged you is no longer alive or they are gone forever into some distant countries or even are unwilling to communicate. These are the times when we have to look deep within us and just forgive.

THE FORGIVENESS WORKOUT

Do you have someone that you would like to forgive? Write down the details of that person and the circumstance necessitating the forgiveness below. Are you ready to let go and forgive? If so, you can proceed to the next step.

Go through the four steps of forgiveness as outlined above. When you feel that you are ready and willing to forgive, fill the following forgiveness statement.

I   do hereby grant wholehearted forgiveness to   .
I consciously extend you my forgiveness for:

To make your forgiveness complete, this is the communication that you have to deliberately make:

It is imperative to talk to your children about the importance of forgiveness. Ask them if they have anyone in their lives that they need to extend forgiveness to. If that is the case, you can take them through the four steps and afterward give them the forgiveness statement and let them fill out.

" WHEN YOU FORGIVE SOMEBODY WHO HAS WRONGED YOU, YOU'RE SPARED THE DISMAL CORROSION OF BITTERNESS AND WOUNDED PRIDE. FOR BOTH PARTIES, FORGIVENESS MEANS THE FREEDOM AGAIN TO BE AT PEACE INSIDE THEIR OWN SKINS AND TO BE GLAD IN EACH OTHERS' PRESENCE. "

- Fredrick Buechner -

Nelson Mandela, the first black and democratically elected President of South Africa once said," *"Resentment is like drinking poison and then hoping it will kill your enemies."* The power to change all that is within you. Peace is a sum total of the decisions we make however small they are, the actions we take however insignificant they are in every micro moment of our lives. The responsibility that lies squarely on our shoulders at the moment is that of creating peace through the power of forgiveness.

LOVE ENCOURAGES AND STRENGTHENS

I am considered by many as an encourager. I always look for the best in a person and the situation. I also look for ways they can be strengthen from the situation, what they could extract and learn from and how to have a positive outlook on life at all times. When you encourage someone it is a very powerful and self-rewarding feeling.

Because I am a very straight forward person I literally just say it. People are often times shocked by how forward and honest I am. To look inside someone and see so much potential that they do not even see in themselves and tell them about it. I love to paint the picture...if you can dream it you can achieve it.

Negativity does not exist in my vocabulary or makeup and should not reside with you neither. Words and thoughts are very powerful and have true meaning and action behind it. When you think negative you get negative when you think positive you get positive or a lesson than need to be learned. Either way it is for your benefit to think positive and speak positive words at all times.

Eliminate words such as "but" "what if" "maybe" etc. Learn to encourage yourself first and then it will become much easier to encourage others. Use words like "I can" "I will" "It shall" and watch the things you think and speak start to happen around you.

An important element of being part of a family, community and society is encouragement. Everyone out there is trying to do their best and by encouraging them, you are literally giving them a new lease of life, an assurance that they are not alone in their daily struggles of life. Encouragement is also an expression that affirms that you appreciate what others are doing and that you would love them to keep on keeping on.

By applauding success, you acknowledge that people matter and their efforts form a significant part of your life. This is regardless of the fact that the person could be stranger or well known to you.

I have a friend who recently lost her son in a violent, unexpected way at such a young tender age of 17. When I received the phone call I immediately thought about her sweet spirit and how devastating this must be on her.

> " WE CAN'T BE AFRAID OF CHANGE. YOU MAY FEEL VERY SECURE IN THE POND THAT YOU ARE IN, BUT IF YOU NEVER VENTURE OUT OF IT, YOU WILL NEVER KNOW THAT THERE IS SUCH A THING AS AN OCEAN, A SEA. HOLDING ONTO SOMETHING THAT IS GOOD FOR YOU NOW, MAY BE THE VERY REASON WHY YOU DON'T HAVE SOMETHING BETTER. "
> - C. JoyBell C. -

What do I say? How do I comfort her? How can I possibly know what to say and I have never experienced it? I simply called and really had no words but I am truly sorry this has happened to her son, her and the family in a tragic murder.

She and I normally have the same vibes and I just felt the anguish and pain that words could not describe. I let her know that I was there for her and asked if she was up for some company as I wanted to respect her space.

She allowed me and my daughter to go over and we cooked a nice meal for the entire family, took a plant and just sat with her. We listened to her talk about her son and the love and compassion she have for her children is awe-inspiring.

I was there for her in any way that she needed me to be and she has thanked me many times for it. Not that she have to thank me but she is a humble, supportive, appreciative woman. I found a true friend for life in her and was glad I was able to be there for her then and now as it is still very new and fresh.

" OUR CHIEF WANT IS SOMEONE WHO WILL INSPIRE US TO BE WHAT WE KNOW WE COULD BE. "
- Ralph Waldo Emerson -

Everyone have their low and high moments. Disappointments in life come to every one of us; it could be as a result of a tight work schedule, failed attempts at work or school, financial difficulties or even health problems. These can be potential sources of frustration and discouragement.

Our words can be that magic wand that will cheer up and speak encouragement into the life of another person who could be scaling terrains of difficulties. Encouragement helps in giving ounces of energy and courage to allow people who feel low and discouraged to face their present and future with confidence and optimism.

However, encouragement is easier said than done. At times you may really feel obligated to step in and help but the mere fact that the situation the other person is going through is strange to you can make it difficult for you to intervene. You could be totally lost for words. Lack of knowledge of the other person's circumstances may hinder us from commenting on the specifics. Here are 10 phrases that can come in handy when you find yourself in such a situation. They can help in bringing a new dimension into the life of the other person.

1. "I AM AVAILABLE IF YOU NEED TO TALK"

One of the ways that can bring relief to a discouraged soul is through the knowledge that someone else has gone to the extent of offering a listening ear and that they are available just for them. You may not be in a position to give sound advice as you would love to but just being around to listen and to try to see things from the other persons perspective can be a powerful remedy. What the discouraged persons need at times is just to talk over their problems with someone else. This can go a long way into giving them the insight that they need to be able to confront the situation facing them.

2. "YOU'VE MADE COMMENDABLE PROGRESS"

Discouraged people rarely notice anything good with their lives. The progress and achievements they have managed to attain can seem so insignificant to them that they easily overlook them. Coming into the picture and opening their eyes to the bits and pieces of success that they have managed to attain can bring back the lost joy and hope in their lives. Let them acknowledge their personal growth, accomplishments and any new habits that they have developed. You may say something like, "I am happy with your workout discipline! You would have said you never could have done this before." I would also say to them "congratulations and continue to celebrate every milestone."

Be careful to isolate and point out positive trends that you have seen in your friends such as how they relate with others. If you know for instance that your friends used to struggle with time management, you can tell them something like, "I have noticed the way you manage your time, you have challenged me completely!" Help them see the positive side rather than the negative side of their lives.

DISCOURAGED PEOPLE RARELY NOTICE ANYTHING GOOD WITH THEIR LIVES

3. "I AM WITH YOU IN THIS"

This phrasal expression reaffirms that whatever the other person is going through, they are not alone and you are with them through each and every phase of their difficulties. Reassure the discouraged party that you want the best out of them and that you are praying for their situation. Make them see that they are not the only ones going through that particular issue. If you are aware of any other person who could have successfully gone through a similar situation, you can suggest that they meet so as to talk further on the circumstance at hand. This will help fight any feelings of solitude and start to look at their situation constructively.

4. "YOU REALLY INSPIRE ME FOR. . ."

A person going through depression and discouragement may lose track of their strengths and unique qualities. By telling them that they encourage you, you make them realize that not all is gone. By pointing out the other persons genuine strengths, you give them a reason to look at themselves again in a positive and optimistic perspective. You need to go beyond their look and personality into their strengths and abilities. Let them know that they are dependable, loving, trustworthy, sincere and patient. If possible, highlight the impact that the person has made in the lives of others. Statements like, "I love your level of organization and order...I can pay for it!" can awaken a downtrodden soul.

5. "THE FUTURE IS BRIGHTER THAN THE PRESENT"

People who are discouraged tend to focus more on the present and lose track of their future. When speaking to such people, you need to teleport them from their current situation and let them have a glimpse of what the future holds for them. You have to help in realizing that in the future they will be able to function a lot better than they are doing currently. By asking soul searching questions such as "is there something You would love to do next year that you are not able to do right now?" you can even help them put down their goals for the future. Be very keen and listen to statements that express his inner desire such as 'I have always wanted to... I wish I had...' excite them along their desired goals and plans and let them know that they can achieve them. Shepherded them along the rails of hope and point to them how bright their future is.

6. "YOUR'RE NOT A FAILURE"

At the lowest point, everyone feels like they are a total failure and mess. This is when disappointment creeps in and makes the situation even worse. Whenever you remind them that they are not failures but rather successful people, you introduce a ray of hope and self confidence in their lives. In case you went through a similar situation in your life, it would do the other person better if you let them know. Be open to speak about what you were feeling back then and even share with them the things that kept you on track despite all that. Encourage him that it is normal to feel downcast and disappointed but we should not let such feelings ruin our lives, we have a living hope.

7. "I WANT TO HELP IN ANY WAY I CAN"

In times of discouragement, help is highly appreciated however small it may be. Offering to help literally takes off the burdens from the other person and as a result, they feel lighter and the journey manageable. You need to know that the other person may feel uncomfortable asking for assistance and therefore you have to be proactive. You can offer to take the children out somewhere just to have fun. You can ask him whether they would like you to go and get them some grocery or have their clothes dry-cleaned. There are lots of other small chores such as cooking or watering her garden that could have a significant impact in her life. Try to put yourself in his/her shoes and try to anticipate the kind of things you would have them do.

8. "THERE IS A SOLUTION TO THIS"

People who are discouraged usually have some hopelessness that tends to roll over them. They may not be able to see the resources that are available at hand to help them in sorting out their problems. By showing them or reaffirming that there is a solution to whatever it is that they are going through, you are helping them to see a new dimension to their problem. You can sit together with them and brainstorm on the possible solutions to the problem at hand. Be ready to incorporate even solutions that may look silly and farfetched. They will help open up hope and revive the conscience. Once in a while laugh the problem off and figure out the best plan out of this.

9. "YOU DID AMAZINGLY WELL"

Failure or a past mistake can clog the centre of reasoning of a discouraged person. Finding something to cheer him up on can be the panacea that will relive him of all his troubles. Applaud him in ways like' "you did a fantastic job". "You are really impressive! That was a record finish." Do not overlook the small things that make the whole emotional clock tick. Compliment hard work and every single initiative, effort or idea. This will restore lost confidence and hype in SELF.

10. "YOU ARE SO SPECIAL AND INDISPENSABLE"

The only person that has abilities and opportunities as unique as your friend is only him. There is no one else in this life and even that to come that can be compared to them. They are fearfully and wonderfully made. No one can duplicate his sense of humor and personality except them. The combination of talents, personality and insights are so uniquely engraved in him that despite his troubles and discouragement, they can only but reside in him. Show him that he is truly special and indispensable and do not let him look down upon himself. Make them aware that you consider spending time with them a privilege.

You need to be truthful with your encouragement. Never say that things will be fine if they really are not. Speak the fact as they are but season them with hope. Do not give blind assurances. Telling them that things are fine while they see clearly that everything is going its own direction will not help the discouraged person. Predict the future within the limits of their expectations. Never tell them of things that are obviously impossible. When such things fail to happen, these people could be disappointed further and even experience higher degree of disillusionment than before.

Focus on the things that are right. This will send signals of care and concern to the person who is discouraged. It will make him aware that despite the suffering or difficulty that he is going through, there are others who are rallying behind him and giving him their backs. This is enough to strengthen them so as to be able to face the setbacks with a positive mindset.

" ENCOURAGEMENT TO OTHERS IS SOMETHING EVERYONE CAN GIVE. SOMEBODY NEEDS WHAT YOU HAVE TO GIVE. IT MAY NOT BE YOUR MONEY; IT MAY BE YOUR TIME. IT MAY BE YOUR LISTENING EAR. IT MAY BE YOUR ARMS TO ENCOURAGE. IT MAY BE YOUR SMILE TO UPLIFT. WHO KNOWS? "

- Joel Osteen -

DIGGING
DEEPER

CHAPTER 5

"In the difficult moments believe in yourself. Believe that you are whole, perfect, powerful, and blessed."
- Debasish Mridha -

LOVE IS FEELING WHOLE AND COMPLETE

" TO BE GREAT, BE WHOLE; EXCLUDE NOTHING, EXAGGERATE NOTHING THAT IS NOT YOU. BE WHOLE IN EVERYTHING. PUT ALL YOU ARE INTO THE SMALLEST THING YOU DO.SO, IN EACH LAKE, THE MOON SHINES WITH SPLENDOR BECAUSE IT BLOOMS UP ABOVE. "

- Fernando Pessoa -

DO YOU FEEL WHOLE AND COMPLETE WITHIN YOURSELF?

This is a very powerful and soul searching question that can expose your inner self if you take it with the interrogation that it instigates inside you. There are two pure and genuine states of being:

1. *The state of inner wholeness*
2. *The state of inner incompleteness*

Your true state of being needs complete honesty on your part as you dialogue with yourself. The state of being incomplete has no permanence and it is a transition that can turn into a state of wholeness if you realize the truth about yourself. It is possible to see and even taste the state of completeness even while you are still in the state of incompleteness. During such circumstances, there is an illusion that makes you cling to the outer and superficial experience, thereby crediting it for the feeling of completeness that you have. However, this is a false belief because the real issue is that you experienced the state of completeness when you temporarily let go of your resistance.

Whenever you experience a fleeting sense of completeness within you, it shows that you are still rooted in your state of incompleteness. Unlike the state of incompleteness, the state of inner completeness has permanence and whenever it comes into you, you will never feel incomplete again, despite your prevailing circumstances.

The life experience that you have when operating from a state of inner incompleteness is fundamentally different from the experience you have when you are operating from a state of inner completeness. From the outside, the difference may not be visible but the details are within. You could be doing the same things on the outside, however, what sets you apart in each of the states is how you generally experience life from within. When you are in the state of inner completeness, you do not move or do things out of the need to feel complete and your driving force is the need to feel inspired at that very moment.

THE REASON BEHIND INNER INCOMPLETENESS

The state of inner incompleteness develops earlier in life approximately at the age of 4 when your focus shifts to your physical. The minds created a narrow identity that it uses to identify you. This mental construct is called the "ego structure." By itself, the ego structure serves an important role of making you conscious of the physical experience and when it dominates the mind, it causes a narrow self-perception. This is where the problem starts. When you allow yourself to look at life and the entire universe through the narrow lenses of the ego structure, wisdom fails. This is precisely the reason why ego-powered self-perception transits into a dysfunction of one sort or the other.

There are lots of traits and habits that manifest themselves when you are in a state of inner incompleteness. Some of them are discussed below:

- *You always seek for external approval of what you are doing and your actions are based on this approval.*

- *There is a state of "craving" inside you that results from the delusion that when you get the thing you are really looking for, you will find rest and be at peace with yourself. There is an energy that drives you towards obsessions and desperations of some sort that emanate from your sense of incompleteness. This creates inner suffering and makes your entire being vibrate because of lack.*

- *You tend to experience temporal and fleeting moments of peace that sooner than later, become clouded with the painful feeling of inner incompleteness.*

- *There is a sense of instability within you occasioned by the volatile motions within your mental chamber.*

- *You will tend to experience a background of irritation, unease and frustration that you may end up blaming the outside forces for while the problem is internal.*

- *There is a constant torment from your physical and mental realms that you may cause exhaustion thereby looking for a way out.*

The strength of the connection between your identification and your ego will determine how narrow your self-awareness is. The stronger the connection the narrower the perception of SELF there is. In other words you are disconnecting with your inner sense of completeness and uniting with your narrow ego centric perception of SELF. By design, the physical realm does not have the capacity to take you to the point of internal completeness because it is temporal, fleeting and incomplete by nature. With time, it becomes dissolved and changes to another form. The physical realm creates fear and anxiety within you.

ATTAINING INNER COMPLETENESS

Due to the fact that the mind through the ego structure created a connection with your identity, you will need to disconnect and desynchronize the mental motions if you are to return to the state of wholeness. The truth is that the process of disconnection takes time; it's purely an internal and conscious deliberation. From the age of around 4 years, your identity has been superimposed on your mental ego structure and to unplug it from here, you will need some time. You need to understand and appreciate the process of returning to inner wholeness so that you can allow it to take place smoothly without creating barriers and pitfalls that may bring it to a halt.

The physical realm, functions more efficiently when you are in the state of inner completeness. You physicality never shies away from total expression and there is no pressure to feel more whole than you are. At this state, there is a background of peace and contentment irrespective of the surrounding circumstances. This environment of inner wholeness gives room for wisdom and well-being to thrive and permeate every aspect of your physical realm. There is always some free energy around and about you.

There is a danger that comes when you try to reason how this state will be or feels like. The mind has a way of constructing some unreal scenarios and states that may give you a false

" THE WHOLE TRUTH IS THIS: THE
TIME OF THE HALF-LIFE IS OVER.
DONE. THERE'S NO MORE TIME
FOR HALF-HEARTED LIVING, HALF-
TRUTHS AND DIVIDING LIFE INTO NEAT
COMPARTMENTS. WE HAVE WORK TO DO
HERE. IT BEGINS FROM THE INSIDE-OUT,
WITH A COMMITMENT TO SEE OURSELVES
AS WHOLE AND TO EMBRACE THE
FULLNESS OF WHO WE ARE AND WHO WE
ARE BECOMING. "

- Dawn Richerson -

opinion on how it is when you attain the state of wholeness. The mental picture that may come to you could be that of unending highs or constant motions of exhilarations. These are just but temporary states of excitement. Wholeness has nothing to do with these surface ripples. In fact, people pursuing such states end up in frustration and with disappointments. Inner completeness is very ordinary, simple in form and structured. It does not come with pomp and color; it is the undisturbed calmness that springs from within.

WHAT DO YOU REQUIRE TO FEEL COMPLETE?

What is it that you possess?
What do you have full control over?

What are your responsibilities?
What is in your store, your garage, your closet?

We are wired to feel secure by what we possess. The mind creates a poignant awareness that you may need this or that the in next minute or in future. It is common to have thoughts such as, "I think I need that," or, "I should not get rid of this," or even, "I still remember when I bought this," and also, "how will they see me if I don't get that."

WE ARE WIRED TO FEEL SECURE BY WHAT WE POSSESS. THE MIND CREATES A POIGNANT AWARENESS THAT YOU MAY NEED THIS OR THAT THE NEXT MINUTE OR IN FUTURE.

All these issues pamper and pad our ego structure while bringing down our spirits. When we lose touch with our real inner selves, we tend to hold onto whatever there is that will give us temporal sense of wholeness. Looking at it critically, having all these things in order to feel complete drains us, along with our entire pool of resources. It takes a considerable amount of energy and time to move, think and maintain all these things. All this happens at the expense of living our normal complete lives.

Any attempt to amass these things with the hope of feeling complete at the end of it all, saddles us with even more stories of incompleteness and desperation. "If I get this, I will end up attaining that," or, "what will happen when I use all of this?"

All of these examples can be termed as the lies of the ego and stories concerning which are made up and unreal. We do not need all of these things to live a complete and amazing life.

HOW TO LIVE A LIFE OF COMPLETENESS WITHOUT OWNING ALL THESE THINGS

1. REALIZE YOUR INNER ABUNDANCE

This may sound ironical, but the reality is that the more you have the less abundant you feel. We usually gather things up so that we can try to fix an inner sense of lack. We always seek to increase ourselves by what we possess. The great news is that you can change your mindset from a state of lack to state of abundance. You have to consciously tell yourself that what you could possibly require is already deposited inside you. Your spirit is aware of this fact and the more you speak positive affirmations to yourself, the more you invalidate your ego-driven propositions.

One of the excellent ways of cancelling your sense of lack is by writing down a gratitude list on a daily basis. Make this a fun-filled experience! When you increasingly become grateful, you also grow and nature the feeling of inner abundance.

THE MORE YOU HAVE THE LESS ABUNDANT YOU FEEL.

1. CONFRONT YOUR FEARS WITH THE LIGHT OF TRUTH

When you dialogue within yourself "I think someday I may require this," you are creating an imagined future which may or may not come to pass. You also need to tell yourself, "I think I will have the capacity to get it then...no need to worry about that now". The moment you identify and illuminate the fear that hangs behind the physical things you desire, in that very moment, it dissolves and vanishes. The next time you experience a craving for something; do not focus on the item itself focus on the fear of not having it.

You can laugh loudly at your ego because it will always make up stories that can push you into doing some great things.

2. BE HONEST WITH YOURSELF AS FAR AS YOUR NEEDS ARE CONCERNED

Everyone wants to feel loved, whole and happy. Research shows that everything we buy, own or want comes from this burning desire. The reality is that nothing we own makes us whole or complete. In fact, they are just stories that purportedly give us little confidence.

Take a moment and look back at the times when you felt really jubilant and alive. There is a great likelihood that those were the moments when you were with someone you cherish or you were doing an exercise that you really loved. This is exactly what we need and there is nothing much that we require aside from this. What we truly need is not the fancy cars and bigger houses, but rather the need to be loved and appreciated by others. Our ego structures have a way of exaggerating things to make them a must and necessities in our lives.

Every time you get occupied with things, what you are essentially doing is nursing your ego. Your true self has no business with those things. The needs of the spirit are just simple, to connect, love and play. Whenever you find yourself in a situation where you are being carried away by things around you, take a moment and focus on yourself; remember that with or without those things, you are whole.

GIVE TO OTHERS WHAT YOU REALLY WANT AND IT SHALL COME BACK TO YOU

This is the central tenet in the discipline of giving and self-sacrifice. When we give others acceptance and love, through spending time with family and friends, giving them a listening ear, having adventures and experience with others, we shall exactly receive back what our inner selves are yearning for in life. When other people spend time with us, there is a high likelihood that we shall reciprocate or feel indebted to reciprocate that. Our lives get a new dimension as we explore and have fun with new things. This effectively breaks the chains that connect our egos to our true identity making us realize how complete and whole we are. The only person who can make you feel complete is yourself.

Banking on others to make you complete is like eating non-food substances with an aim of becoming nutritionally satisfied. You could become full but that is only temporal. The problem of hunger can only be addressed comprehensively by food. Using others to attain self-completion can be counterproductive and frustrating.

Every time we feel incomplete, we tend to look for other people that can plug in and fill the gap to make us whole. But because they are not the solution, we end up with an endless craving that leaves us embarrassed and disappointed.

To be able to visualize the difference between needing and wanting someone or their attention, look at a beggar dressed in tatters, hungry and screaming for change, compared to a well-dressed or fine looking person inviting you to an evening party.

Don't mistake me, there is no offense in wanting others, this however should come after you attain inner completeness. Other than that, you will just be looking for bits and pieces to complete the inner puzzle. The person inviting you to the party is complete and they can function without you as opposed to the beggar who could even die if they do not get the change.

The first step therefore is to be comfortable with yourself. An incomplete person tends to feel scared whenever they get into inner dialogue with themselves.

It is always good to have people around you to enjoy the company of one another but never do this in lieu of running away from SELF. You need to spend quality time with yourself if you are to start the journey to inner wholeness.

Some people fear spending time alone because they cannot stand the shock and horror of their own lives. They start thinking about their past and present lives. This is however one of the ways in which you break loses so keep on that trajectory and never back off.

When you get to the level of being comfortable with yourself, you do not need much time to yourself every day; just a bit of it can be such a nice treat. "Me time" is an excellent opportunity for you to think about the path that your life is taking and the goals that lie ahead of you. It's also a wonderful time to just be with the most cherished person in your life, yourself!

Exploring yourself fully in terms of your goals, your unique qualities, your identity and so forth needs time. There is a whole lot of exciting and damning things that you need to know about yourself; this is the only way you can truly appreciate who you are. You need to be aware of your true needs and wants other than desiring the needs of others.

For those people who get married early in their lives, they tend to miss this part of their lives. Having someone in your life with their own set of needs and wants can make it very difficult to hear yourself clearly.

HOW TO ATTAIN SELF-COMFORT

There are a few ways through which you can enjoy your own company and learn more about yourself.

- Spend 5 minutes writing down all the things you admire about yourself, get a piece of paper or notebook and write. Never stop writing, even when you run short of ideas. Write until the 5 minutes are over. This exercise will open up your loving and caring eyes to yourself.

- Recollect all the bad incidences, troubles and insecurities you overcame, we always think of the juicy and rosy experiences and tend to shut our memory on the bad experiences. You need to be fair to yourself and roll down your memory window to uncover the bad experiences you had. The same way you overcame them will be the same manner in which you will triumph over the current ones. This will give you rest, comfort and assurance.

- Have a "date" with yourself, plan a nice treat for yourself such as a hot bath and massage. Have a drink while watching the sun setting beyond the rolling plains. Be creative in this; watching a good movie can be an excellent idea. This will create familiarity between you and your SELF.

ATTAINING NEW HAPPINESS IN INNER COMPLETION

There is happiness that is beyond sorrow and conflict. Getting to this kind of happiness however requires that you first be whole. Any happiness that exists apart from self-wholeness is half baked, temporal and transient.

BE YOURSELF AND BE COMPLETE

Whenever we find ourselves running up and down looking for other things outside ourselves to make us complete, we should stop and question the force behind all this. The only power that can compel us to move heaven and earth in search of things that will make us happy can only be the emptiness that comes with being incomplete.

In our natural settings, none of us can be pushed to the point of destruction in order to complete ourselves. It only happens when there is a powerful force within us that misinforms and misdirects us into a misplaced sense of incompleteness.

Our lives are majorly shaped by the will and power of what is incomplete within us. Often, we deny this fact and we convince ourselves through logical explanation and well thought out rationales. We have to come into terms with this will and how it stealthily operates within us to rob us of the consciousness of being complete.

The root of temptation lies in the fact that we are constantly trying to fulfill an inner sense of emptiness through things that are conceptualized out of deception. The inner state of Incompleteness orders some things that we erroneously believe that will make us incomplete, only to find out that they are not the magic. The struggles that we find ourselves entangled in geared towards completing our inner selves can be rightfully traced to a budding feel of insufficiency and the fear to remain in this state for long unless something or anything is done to relieve us of this insatiable feeling of being incomplete.

To find the source of this incessant urge to complete ourselves, we need to first of all appreciate that it resides inside us. Then we need to realize that there are some of our body parts that work in collaboration with this force and even swallow the empty promises that emanate from this unseen nature. While searching for this new order of self-triumph, we need to also realize the truth about our inner experience. Resistance and rebellion will not help us in this.

At one point or the other, we find ourselves doing things while struggling and even hating ourselves for them. After doing whatever it is that we do out of the false compulsion to feel complete, we tend to look down upon ourselves as powerless beings without the resilience to withstand such pressures. We have to be honest and accept that these unwanted events happen to us and within us daily. Some of them are as simple as sleeping for the extra 10 minutes when we know that we should have woken up at the top of the hour. At times we let something undesirable someone has said to roll over in our minds longer than necessary. The bottom line to all this is that we are dragged into doing whatever we do by a force that has its own makeup. And that all these compulsive behaviors constitute addiction because their tentacles grab us making us unable to turn off their demands.

At this point in our journey to self, we need to realize that most of these moments are painful and regrettable. They begin with a thought as simple as, "let me just watch the last episode," or "let me eat the last slice". The next point is the realization that you have strayed and are now resenting missed opportunities. You may even be somewhere spending time and money shopping for things that are not really necessary.

This shows that within, there is a resident will that has a nature which constantly tells us how incomplete we are. This is the same nature that drives us to do lots of things in an attempt to fix the thing that makes us incomplete. The beliefs that it puts forward are false and lead to an even larger hole of emptiness and frustration.

" OUR CHIEF WANT IS SOMEONE WHO WILL INSPIRE US TO BE WHAT WE KNOW WE COULD BE. "
- Ralph Waldo Emerson -

When we are under the influence of the pain of incompletion, we are forced from within to believe that we have no other option but to engage in the things that we are forced to indulge in. In doing these things, we are powered by a belief from within us that we shall free ourselves from the shackles of the monster causing self-dissatisfaction. Though unconscious, we pursue these things with a matter of urgency so as to free ourselves from the pain of being incomplete.

One of the things that we have to understand is that if we need to awaken ourselves and break off from this vicious cycle of addiction and all its related behaviors, we have to know ourselves more and how the inner deception mechanism

works. The process may be summarized as below.
The dark will resides in us and its activities dominate our decision making processes and has impact on out power to discern. This will searches the highs and the lows within and without us so as to end its sense of emptiness. This will is part of our incomplete nature that cannot find enough to satisfy it and is always at war with its craving desires that extend to material needs.

The truth of our spiritual standing can only be seen in the one way and there is no substitute for it. Self-seeing is the source of the strength that we need to break off from the thought pattern that makes us feel incomplete. However, if we really wish to know and experience this kind of power, we need to enter the inner chambers where the battle is raging. This power is the gift of grace that comes upon us as we long to see ourselves whole and complete.

Instead of being taken hostage by the power that brings in the need to fulfill yourself through material cravings, you need to stand up and claim what rightfully belongs to you; the sense and feel of completeness. Wake up, repossess your control and shake off the shackles of the monstrous desires that have taken you captive. If you do this, you will experience the enriching and relaxing feel of being independent. Up until now when you reclaimed your attention and conscious sense of SELF, your sense incompleteness had taken full control of you and you were totally sold to it. The new dispensation however sets a clear path which leads to a reconciliation with your inner completeness just like it was at the beginning.

While remaining conscious and wide awake to the things that your redeemed attention has revealed to you, you need to deliberately shift your focus so as to remain steadfast to what your Heart knows it's true; your complete self. You also have to realize that the gripping and deceptive force that has made you suffer in pain for believing that you are incomplete if far from giving up. The encouragement however, is that your inner determination to pursue your complete SELF is stronger and can make you overcome. You are at the driving seat of your own course of action; never lose focus.

In addition, give your attention and direct your energy to what you know for sure. Doing this will make you complete and cannot be taken away through deception and empty promises by the incomplete self. This deliberate and conscious move will give you the strength and the power required to break forth and be free. Now that you know the truth of your inner situation, your attention is no longer on the feeling of being incomplete and you are convinced that the niceties that the incomplete self suggests `cannot quench the desire to be complete.

Our next phase in the pursuit of the state of inner completeness comes into truth once we remember and acknowledge what is whole and bring in the awareness of God who is the Greatest Truth and the Light into our mind. Once this paradigm shift has occurred and we take our place on the redemptive seat of personal awareness, we slowly begin to surrender ourselves to the goodness and sense of completeness that though we may not feel at the moment, we know that it is slowly taking root in us. We relinquish our entire will to it; we immerse ourselves completely in its healing waters so that we can fully realize how complete and whole we are.

ATTRACTING
MORE POSITIVE

CHAPTER 6

"If someone thinks that peace and love
are just a cliche that must have been
left behind in the 60s, that's a problem.
Peace and love are eternal."

- John Lennon -

LOVE IS PEACE AND COMPASSION

War! War! War! War! That is all we hear these days. One country battling against one another for stupid selfish reasons and do not take the people interests to heart at all.

Why do we live in a world with so much chaos and destruction going on? Why are we allowing it to happen? Do you not have a voice anymore or did you forget that you really were created to be "FREE"! Everybody and everything is at war with each other.

" WHEN THE POWER OF LOVE OVERCOMES THE LOVE OF POWER THE WORLD WILL KNOW PEACE. "
- Jimi Hendrix -

It is this negative energy that we are creating and putting out into the atmosphere that is causing self-destruction. It is time for YOU to wake up. Yes you...the one who is reading this book right now. What can you do for your community? How are you contributing to world peace? Do you support war?

I wonder how different the world will be if we all lived in peace, harmony and showed compassion and love towards one another. Most will say that is wishful thinking, but imagine if we all did our part individually, that would add up as a whole by creating positive energy and a thriving environment.

We are at war in our homes, on jobs, in schools, with family members, neighbors, religions and the list goes on. If we took less time and energy creating negative energy, we could devote that to positive energy. Imagine that! The world will have a very powerful shift!

" IF HUMANITY IS TO PROGRESS, GANDHI IS INESCAPABLE. HE LIVED, THOUGHT, ACTED AND INSPIRED BY THE VISION OF HUMANITY EVOLVING TOWARD A WORLD OF PEACE AND HARMONY. "

- Dr. Martin Luther King Jr. -

Peace has often been misconstrued as an external state of being where we live in harmony with others. Others have even gone to the extent of saying that peace belongs to the hippies. When all is said and done, there are two dimensions to peace that we must realize and appreciate; the inward perspective and the outward dimension. When we talk of the inward, we mean our hearts and minds. This is the source of the internal impulse that causes us to move towards violence. Without taming and controlling our inner self, the storm within will ultimately spill to the outside.

According to your beliefs and lifestyle, you will find a peaceful co-existence within yourself and even with the external factors you interact with. There is however some basics that cannot be overlooked if the path to peace is to be fully realized. Some of these factors are tolerance, non-violence, celebration of life and ascribing to moderate views. In the discussions that will ensue, we shall look at the elements that will help you in discovering your journey to peaceful co-existence. A way of life only you can be directly responsible for its success.

LOVE OTHERS AND DO NOT SEEK TO CONTROL THEM

The first step towards a life of peace is to stop the quest to exercise power over others. Controlling people means that you want to impose your will on them without getting into their universe so as to share their perspective to issues. Any approach to relationship that incorporates an element of control will put you in a collision path with others. To experience true peace, you need to replace the will to control with a desire to love unconditionally. Appreciate and accept people together with their weaknesses and strengths.

Let peace lead then power to follow- Mahatma Gandhi once said that power that is buttressed on love is much more effective and permanent that power that is seized through threats and punishment. Getting control of power through threats will give you subjects that act out of coercion and not respect for your stature. This is not the path to peaceful coexistence.

Master the art of negotiation, assertive communication and conflict resolution- these skills are indispensable if you are to operate effectively even through conflict. It is not always that we will steer clear of conflict but knowing how to skillfully handle it can be such a great thing. Just like other skills, it is possible to learn these skills through research and study. Clarity in communication can significantly reduce conflict because most of the misunderstandings come from vague communications.

While in communication with others, you need to steer clear of tendencies that will amount to demands, threats, or ordering. These traits can easily give rise to conflict with the people around you as they may think that you are trying to control them as opposed to interacting on the same platform.

CONFIDENCE!
CONFIDENCE!
CONFIDENCE!

Having confidence within yourself, and with those around you, means that you can be able to live a good life ceteris paribus is such a refreshing feeling. Reasoning along the same vein and when giving advice, you can share more of your insights and your perspective, rather than instructing the other person on the way they ought to live.

The latter may amount to interference with the other person's life. According to Dag Hammerskjold, a Swedish diplomat, *"Not knowing the question, it was easy to give an answer."* At times when we advise other people, we miss out on the crux of the matter and as such we tend to wobble solutions that do not fully address the problem at hand. We align things from our perspectives without considering the dimension of the other person. It will do more good, to respect the intelligence of the other person and just be there for them rather than imposing our own will. Doing this will enable you to cultivate peace, respect and confidence for the other people.

LEARN HOW
TO MODERATE
YOUR CONVICTIONS

Thinking in absolute patterns and holding to convictions without giving space and chance to the other person to express their points of view is a sure way of attracting conflict in your life. Convictions bring into the picture extremist thinking that usually leads to hasty and reactive driven habits that are devoid of reflective and deliberate thinking. This kind of thinking is always criticized because it brings in a false state of confidence and act as a hindrance to the realities in the world around us. This leads us into conflict the moment other people fail to concur with our reasoning. Having a stand developed out of conviction makes it difficult for you to be open-minded and appreciative of any reviews of your understanding that could have an immediate and long-term benefit. This in turn hinders your ability to live in harmony with others.

Having convictions is not bad but you should learn how to moderate them. This will soften your reasoning and give dialogue a chance making it easy for you to reflect and question. You need to realize that the passion, belief, opinions and faith that you have is just a subset of what the world has. Cultivate a habit of moderation that values worth and human dignity.

FOLLOW THE GOLDEN RULE

Treat others as you would want to be treated.

Whenever you feel that there is a tendency of extremism developing in you, engage in lots of activities and meeting with lots of people. It is hard and almost impossible to slip into extreme convictions when leading such a lifestyle.

DEVELOP A SENSE OF HUMOR

Humor is a charm that draws people towards peace. Some people tend to be so busy with their lifestyles that they take their work and career too seriously. Humor helps in releasing tension and undercuts tendencies of extremist thinking.

CULTIVATE TOLERANCE

When you exercise tolerance in all that you engage in, you will soon make a difference both in your life and the lives of others. Tolerance means appreciating diversity, living and letting others live and also valuing the plurality of society. The moment we fail in tolerating others beliefs, opinions, value systems and ways of thinking we shall slowly find ourselves sliding into dehumanization, discrimination, depression and finally violence. By exercising tolerance you are setting the stage for a peaceful life.

Resist the urge of jumping into conclusions about others and shift your perspective to start cherishing what others have to offer. Through your changed perspective towards other people, you also can be an integral player in the initiation of change in the lives of others. A good example would be to stop seeing other people as stupid and incompetent to start seeing them as effective, instrumental and intelligent. This will serve as nourishment and an encouragement to them to live up to the expectation you have for them. Seeing others as being clever, special, interesting and caring despite their anger, bravado and torment can bring a great revolution in their lives.

BE PEACEFUL

The Indian Legendary Mahatma Gandhi said, *"There are many causes that I am prepared to die for but no cause that I am prepared to kill for."* Peaceful people do not and cannot cause violence and pain on others not even animals. Despite the violence that is being perpetrated all over the world you need to develop a philosophy that steers clear of death and murder.

Every time a person tries to arm-twist you into believing that violence is permissible, you need to stick to your value system and shun away from such. There will be people who will castigate you for being peaceful and insinuating that you are undermining people involved in conflict zones. This should however not move you because you clearly know that violence and conflict that leaves scores of people dead, injured and displaced has no place in the society. Mary Robinson, the former UN High Commissioner for Human Rights, once said, *"My experience of conflict is that those who are involved in it long for even a day of peace. To have a day of cessation of violence, that to me is an idea whose time has come."* You need to be a firm believer of the fact that violence is not plausible not even to those who are involved in it. Peace is the ultimate longing of every heart and soul.

Being at peace means to act with compassion especially towards those who perpetrate violence. Criminals too deserve to know what it means to be peaceful. On the contrary however the society we live in tortures, incarcerates, and gives space for violence to thrive in our prisons. This makes us no different even to those we label as criminals. We need to demonstrate by actions what peace is all about not just paying lip service.

Try to stay away from violent movies, music that has degrading lyrics and news reports that carry violent scenes.

Surround yourself with symbols and emblems of peace such as peaceful music, images and even people. Peace is contagious and the more you are around it, the more it infuses into your system.

Consider living a life of vegetarianism or veganism in future. This will make you be at peace with animals. Take time to do research on how animals are treated in abattoirs, farms and pharmaceuticals then you will have a clearer picture on how to align your beliefs with the sentient beings. Correlate everything you learn out of this and your need to live a peaceful life.

ENGAGE IN THOUGHT REFLECTION

Hasty responses without time to reflect and ponder on the complexity of the issue in question is not beneficial. You need to think over all the angles and dimensions before giving your word. This will limit the chances of coming up with a tragic outcome. It is understandable that there are times when a quick response is necessary. These times however are fewer compared to the many instances an issue gives room and for careful consideration. Better outcomes can only result from well thought out responses.

When you are hurt either physically or mentally, desist from acting out of anger or violence. Stop first and think. A peaceful response avails much.

Be responsible enough and ask the other person to stop and think before they act. Anger and violence cannot resolve a conflict but rather they inflame it. If the other party insists that violence is the way out, slowly remove yourself from such a situation.

STOP YOURSELF

Whenever you feel that you want to react to something out of anger, stop and remove your SELF from the situation at hand so that you can avoid the confusion and irritation. This will give you space to overcome the feelings of anger and instead replace them with solutions generated out of thoughtfulness.

DEVELOP REFLECTIVE LISTENING

The spoken word can be erroneous and misleading. Many times, people who are angry tend to speak things that are not exactly what they would like to express. In addressing a situation such as this, John Powell said, *"In true listening, we reach behind the words; see through them, to find the person who is being revealed. Listening is a search to find the treasure of the true person as revealed verbally and non-verbally."* Reflective thinking helps in seeing people from another dimension rather than our own perspective. It helps in digging down, to what someone is really expressing and meaning. This prevents reactions based on our thinking and guessing.

STOP VENGEANCE, SEEK FORGIVENESS INSTEAD

The eye for an eye approach does not lead to peace but instead it has resulted into injuries and deaths. It is not only pointless but also self-perpetuating to go with this approach given history and the lessons that we have learnt from it. Despite our religious orientation, culture or race, at the bottom of it all we are human beings. We have the same ideologies of raising our families and giving them a good satisfying life. Our differences should not divide us and cause conflict but rather ought to be backbone around which we are united. Reacting to another person in manner that you fill is commensurate to the degree of harm they have inflicted upon you is a sure way of perpetrating violence and hatred. Pursue forgiveness as you seek peace with those who hurt you.

LIVE NOW
NOT IN THE PAST

It is rather given that at some point in the course of our lives, we may have been hurt by someone close or around us. While the action cannot be reversed, you can choose to let go what happened through forgiveness. Forgiveness gives you the opportunity to live in the present even as you look forward into the future. This is the ultimate victory as you reconcile with your past and start to enjoy life again without thinking about the bruises you suffered.

WHEN YOU FORGIVE, YOU LET
GO OF ANY RESENTMENT

When you forgive, you let go of any resentment. You learn how to cope with and control the negative feelings that arose out of you following the incident that made you angry. Forgiveness leads to an acknowledgement of those hurtful feelings instead of burying them under. By forgiving, you gain a unique perspective that enables you to really understand why the other person did what they did, the motivation behind their actions.

By masking your anger, you are releasing yourself into a situation where your independence is taken captive. Rather than speaking and defending the course of justice, you are causing hopelessness by allowing yourself to be trapped in your emotions. Whenever you are addressing a situation where someone else claims that their honor was interfered with, you need to be sober enough so as to let them speak their mind and let forgiveness and understanding champion the cause of peace and resolution. When the worse comes to the worst and you feel forgiveness cannot be given, choose to distance yourself from the matter and do not advocate for violence.

SEARCH FOR INNER PEACE

Whenever inner peace is disrupted, you will be in a constant state of conflict with yourself. Many people, who suffer this lack of inner peace, usually try to look for possessions and things that will fill the gap and bring them peace. These things on the contrary aggravate the situation and lead into a perpetual state of unhappiness. Whenever you find yourself craving for something that you do not have, chances are that you are in an inner state of conflict. While in this situation, you will tend to forget the things that you ought to be grateful for because most of your time is spent in striving to get that car, that house or that post. After you accumulate these things you have cravingly looked for, you will find yourself again in a situation of conflict. This comes especially when the needs of these possessions such as cleaning, security, maintenance and so forth start calling.

Cut back on the things that you long to possess and instead focus on your inner life and the decisions that will make you beautiful.

Whenever you get angry, you can find a quiet place where you just sit and relax. Turning off the computer or television will give you an enabling environment that will allow for meditation and cooling off. Taking a walk is also an option. Get out and explore nature with all it comes along with. Stay in these environments until you feel calm and at peace with yourself then you can resume your normal duties.

Make it a habit that you spend at least 10 minutes daily in a quiet place such as under a tree or in a park. Such an environment brings in a sense order and harmony.

Living in peace cannot be compared to living without violence. Peace means more than just the absence of chaos and anger. Avoid places and situations that will stress you up such as crowds of people and traffic jams.

LIVE JOYFULLY

A perfect anecdote to violence is shifting of your focus to the wonders of the world. It becomes almost impossible to experience fits of rage and be motivated to act violently if you spend your time admiring the amazing, beautiful and wondrous scenes that bring joy and happiness to you. Destruction of innocence and beauty is the greatest despair that is brought about by war and conflict. Joy champions peace because it allows you to see the good that deposited in others and the beauty that the world has.

SABOTAGING YOUR RIGHT TO HAPPINESS

Through feelings of unworthiness and worrying about how others perceive you, you can set a spiral of negative feelings that can rob you of your happiness.

There is more to life than your job. When you do what your heart loves most, you will find satisfaction, joy and happiness.

As much as it is appreciated that your job needs to provide for your livelihood, it is also important that it fulfills your life's vision. Thich Nhat Hanh says, *"Do not live with a vocation that is harmful to humans and nature. Do not invest in companies that deprive others of their chance to life. Select a vocation which helps realize your ideal of compassion."* Based on this guidance, you can make your own decision as per the work that will give you sustenance and peace.

BE THE CHANGE YOU WOULD LOVE TO SEE

This has become a clarion call that stresses the importance of leading by example and not by samples. There are a number of ways through which you can champion this:

- **START BY CHANGING YOURSELF -** the entry point of violence in our lives is when we accept that it can be a solution to our conflicts. This means that the solution to violence is within us. We have to consciously decide to be peaceful. By changing ourselves, everything around us will change too and ultimately the whole world.

- **BE PART OF THE SOLUTION AND NOT THE PROBLEM -** Train yourself to love everybody for whom they are. Try as much as possible to make people comfortable whenever they are around you and give them the chance to be themselves. In this way, you will gain a lot of friends and respect from them.

- **PARTICIPATE IN PEACE INITIATIVES -** make a commitment to celebrate peace worldwide through such days as UN International Day of Peace which is an annually celebrated occasion to marking global ceasefire and non-violence. It's marked every 21 September.

- **DISCUSS WITH OTHERS ABOUT PEACE -** there is power in sharing and discussions. Share with others the ideas that will help enhance peace in the world. Spend time to hear other people's views and perspectives on what peace is. You can either make videos or write stories that you can share with others to communicate the meaning of peace.

- **SACRIFICE AND HELP OTHERS -** It is a noble action that which desires to bring peace into the world through sacrifice and personal initiative. Great leaders such as Mahatma Gandhi sacrificed their legal career in South Africa which was very lucrative in exchange for a life of simplicity as he shared his life with the destitute and less fortunate. He challenged many people and got accolades from every corner of the globe without wielding power and controlling anyone-he was just good. Using the power of altruism you too can bring peace to the entire world through your willingness to sacrifice. By serving causes greater than yourself, you shall win the hearts of millions of people. Volunteering can be the greatest and the simplest way to start.

- **BRING HARMONY BY CHAMPIONING PEACE AND LOVE FOR ALL PEOPLE -** From a distance this may seem like a daunting task. However it can be done. Taking time to reflect on lives of people like Mahatma Gandhi who were fragile and meek in stature but were still able to do so much for mankind. He internalized and practiced the discipline of peace without violence.

SHARE WITH OTHERS THE IDEAS THAT WILL HELP ENHANCE PEACE IN THE WORLD

WIDEN YOUR UNDERSTANDING OF PEACE

The path you choose in life is totally upon you. Writers and philosophers will just show you possible suggestions that you can factor in your life. No one should impose their will on you and make you a salve to their dogmas. Living in peace and coexisting with all people in harmony is ultimately your own deliberate and conscious decision. The things you do or not do on a daily basis, your understanding and beliefs collected from the books you have read and the seminar you have attended will all coalesce to a solid definition of peace in your perspective. Go forth and proclaim peace to all mankind.

KARMA

CHAPTER 7

"How people treat you is their karma;
how you react is yours."
- Wayne W. Dyer -

(Extracted from 21 Essential Lessons)

The Law of Harmony is one of the fundamental laws of Life, upon which all else rests. God, the giver of all life-energy, requires that every electron of such life-energy loaned to man will be qualified in a harmonious manner. Harmony, an action of divine love, requires the continuous pouring forth of kindly feelings of good will to each other. To be in continuous state of harmony, we need to look to the God-Presence I AM and the Ascended Host of Light for guidance, protection, happiness, and PEACE! Let each of say and FEEL. *"God grant us PEACE, and LET IT BEGIN WITH ME."*

THE LAW OF KARMA
The Origin of Karma

Energy is man's to command. Energy becomes power through use, whether through the wielding of a sledge hammer, or I using the God-power almighty to build a momentum of victory, in commanding the electronic light to manifest a decree.

THE LAW OF CAUSE & EFFECT
When the Law of Harmony is broken, this results in karma. The tem "karma" is always used in a negative sense. It shows the recoil of using energy in a discordant manner. If we use energy in a constructive manner, we use the term *"accumulated good."*

The Law of Karma is one of God's universal laws. It is sometimes referred to as the Law of the Circle, the Law of Retribution, or *"what you sow, you reap."* What you place upon your thoughts, feelings, words, and deeds, goes through your own being and world first, and then out to the person, place, condition or thing to which it is directed, but since you are "home" to that life and energy, after it has reached its destination, it begins its journey to you-gathering more of that particular quality or vibration with which it was originally charged. Therefore, you receive back into your world that which you sent forth, amplified whether it was constructive or destructive.

With every thought, feeling, word and act, waking or sleeping, you are creating either your karma of distress or a crown of light.

The Law of Karma was not intended as a threat of punishment of evil-doers, but as an expression of the mathematical precision of life, that one must sow the seed of perfection in concise mathematical accuracy, that the reaping will be in exact proportion to the sowing.

It is not generally understood by mankind that as self-conscious expressions of life, each one is held responsible by Cosmic Law for every particle of this precious energy drawn from the heart of the Godhead.

Every individual has created a certain amount of what is loosely referred to as destructive karma, in his earth life since the fall of man. This karma acts on many places, determined by which body is the chief offender in the case. For instance, the physical body performing acts of violence, (acts of physical assault) releases a tremendous amount of misqualified energy that sooner or later attaches itself to the physical body. Likewise, acts of discord o the mental plane, such as crimes of mental cruelty, result in the mental element being charged with the vibratory action and stamp of the individuals. At some future time these pressures return to the mental body.

Individuals that perform acts of emotional cruelty charge the substance of the emotional plane with certain vibratory actions which will record in the emotional body of the individual.

When a discordant vibration is emitted from an individual, the distance it covers before returning depends on the intensity in which it is projected, both on its outward and on its homeward journey. It obeys the Law of the Circle, and while it is absent from the aura of the individual who is responsible for its projection, it attracts to itself vibrations corresponding to its own rate so that by the time it completes the circle and returns home, it is accompanied by a good number of the same quality of thought and feeling vibrations with which it started.

THE LAW OF CONSERVATION OF ENERGY

According to the Law of Conservation of Energy, all the primal substance (divine energy) must be used wisely. Therefore students should control their speech. Idle chatter and gossip is a waste of God's energy. There is a German proverb that speaks to this. It goes like this, "Before you speak, evaluate if what you are about to say is really needed, useful and truthful."

"The WILL OF GOD is GOOD. The WILL OF GOD is for a free people! The WILL OF GOD is that the axis of the Earth shall be straightened, that the extremes of climate shall be mercifully blended. The WILL OF GOD is that every man, from within himself, shall draw forth the substance and supply which is the need and requirement of his everyday existence. The WILL OF GOD is that there shall be no veil between man and God, and that angels, devas, and all God-free Being shall walk and talk freely with the evolutions of the Earth as men now talk with each other."

"This is the WILL OF GOD: the lame to be made whole, the sick to rise, the diseased to become filled with ease and balance-each one entering into the deep recesses of his heart, facing his own Supreme Divinity, seeing it face to face, and becoming enamored of the magnificent perfection pre-ordained and destined for each lifestream."

"It is time that the WILL OF GOD be impressed with such strength and power into the consciousness of mankind, that there can no longer be any dallying in the shadows nor acceptance of limitation as part of this great Universal First Cause.

The WILL OF GOD is GOOD!
The WILL OF GOD is LIGHT!
The WILL OF GOD is HAPPINESS!
The WILL OF GOD is PEACE!
The WILL OF GOD is PURITY!
The WILL OF GOD is BALANCE!
The WILL OF GOD is KINDNESS!

TRUE WISDOM comes from understanding the laws of life and applying them. This necessitates listening to the Voice of the Silence in humble and silent reverence. The wiser one becomes, the more silent is the tongue, the more peaceful the emotional world, and less thinking is done with the brain. This ray also represents the second person of the Trinity referred to as the "Son," the path of wisdom, of listening and waiting. This is one of the most difficult steps on the path, for until you can hear the Voice of the Silence, you are running on the periphery of life, shouting with the multitude the hollow hosannas that resound nowhere but in your own ears.

"There is a great deal to be said about REVERENCE FOR LIFE, and a great deal to be thought about, for remember- life comes from God, and no matter in what form life functions temporarily, it is pre-ordained to return to God's estate.

"It is easy to reverence an individual, or a few with whom you are in association. "Now you are coming again to an understanding that reverence for life is impersonal and covers the entire human race and all that lives. In learning that, you shall then be the precipitating powers of good! What a small rose can do, surely a human being can do! The rose follows its divine pattern and it blooms in its season. Mankind must come to a point where he or she can reverence the life that is within himself and then, in time, expand it in love until he, too, becomes the Christ manifest, wherever he may be."

"THIS IS THE GREATEST TEACHING THAT THERE IS IN THE THIS WHOLE WORLD, THE GREATEST UNDERSTANDING, THE GREATEST SPIRITUAL LAW THAT THERE IS IN THIS UNIVERSE! LEARN TO REVERENCE LIFE, AND WHEN YOU DO THAT, YOU WILL NOT HURRY, YOU WILL NOT BE BITTER OR DISTRESSED, YOU WILL COME INTO THE GRACEFUL WAY OF LIVING -."

The concentrated power of attention, without which the mind could not conceive or know anything here or hereafter. The power of your attention is the open door to your mind and your entire consciousness.

The qualification of energy creates a CAUSE, that effects is directed into the universe and create an EFFECT, the effect is directed back toward its creator, and the creator's reaction to that effect (emotionally, mentally, etherically, or physically) creates another cause. Thus you have circles within circles. Accepting the return current of energy as having emanated from one's self, the creator then learns quickly that it is wise to send forth only CONSTRUCTIVE CAUSES from his world, and that he should not start a chain reaction whereby a new series of both causes and effects are set into motion. Some earnest souls have misinterpreted this Law by accepting the distressing return of their own misqualified energies and piously saying, "It is God's will!" Others rebel and say that there is no God. Neither of these statements are true, of course, but these are two extremes of human reaction which must be illumined and corrected by the Brotherhood of Truth through patient teaching, counsel and example.

"Every thought and feeling, every virtue and every vice, contribute to a 'mass consciousness' of that particular quality, and into this stratum are constantly pouring the qualified energies of all the intelligences belonging to the evolution. Each individual tunes into and draws from that 'mass consciousness' the particular thought and feelings.

There is a stratum of the Ascended Masters qualities and virtues. LOVE is but one expression of the many divine aspects of this divine consciousness. When an individual is loving, he instantly tunes into the love stratum and becomes one in consciousness with all who love throughout the universe. WISDOM is another, and when an individual seeks wisdom, he is instantly tuned into the vibratory waves of wisdom which are being fed by the divine mind of God and tapped b all the scholars of the world."

"It is also used true of the discordant qualities, and one cannot entertain a thought of jealously, suspicion, hatred, or anger without becoming instantly ONE with the mass stratum of these qualities, as well as with all individuals who are vibrating with similar destructive thoughts and feelings throughout the planet. THE INDIVIDUAL, THROUGH FREE WILL, IS CONSTANTLY RISING AND FALLING THROUGH THESE

VARIOUS STRATA AS THE EMOTIONS AND THOUGHTS FLUCTUATE.

"For example, possessiveness is a tremendous feeling form that draws the God-energy and smothers the object of its affection. Gossip is almost the most insidious because, through poison sent out, it starts whirls of emotion in the lifestreams of many, and soon you have an inner conflagration. What you plant in the mind of another, what grows there as a result, IS YOUR KARMA! Whatever word passes from your lips that pollutes the consciousness of another, is SIN. This is so even if it is based on so-called fact, and whether or not it is spoken in innuendo or outright accusation. Why? Because you thus add to the shadows of the world, and you are not speaking TRUTH! The truth about every man, woman and child on this planet is ONLY GOOD! Whatever imperfection you see in another with your eyes, or hear with your ears, and then pass on to someone else, will make YOU responsible to the great Cosmic Law, and you will have to pay for that in some way!"
"Criticism, condemnation and judgment are also closely related. The silent criticism of seeing discrepancies and faults in others disturbs the feelings of one's own emotional body and sets up causes of discord which react in physical disturbances, but the SPOKEN criticism sets others' emotional bodies into the same vibratory action and its unhappy effects are without limit. The effects of the really vicious emotions of jealousy, hate, anger, and malice are self-evident. The aspiring student should avoid these at all times," (he should either be silent or speak only words of truth).

"Now consciously CONSECRATE:
"Your minds and bodies to receive the divine ideas of the Father – your feelings to radiate that which is helpful, constructive and good, your etheric body to record only perfection, your garment of flesh to manifest health and harmony, your eyes to see perfection and to bless all life, your ears to hear the harmonies of the inner light, the voice of the Master, and the call for assistance from your fellowman, your lips to form the words that carry hope, faith and the confidence of heaven into the consciousness's that are bound, your hands to heal, your feet to walk upon the path as directed by the God who

made you, your heart to be the chalice of the Sacred Fire, and your whole being consecrated and dedicated to God's service. THIS IS MY ACTIVITY TO LIFE!"

"What can be accomplished on Earth, even in mundane activities of your daily living, without concentration, from the smallest task of learning a recipe for your kitchen fare, to the greatest dexterity of technique which produces lovely music, to the greatest development of science, to the magnificent perfection of the educator, preacher and statesman? If there is not concentration, there is only mediocrity, and only the bare surface is scratched. Those who determine to rise above the masses take on facet of living and masterfully develop it – deciding within themselves to excel along at least on line of expression, and according to their concentration is their master and efficiency.

"It is the Law – actual scientific Law – that what you begin CAN BE ACCOMPLISHED when it is in agreement with God's plan to bring perfection forth, whether it is healing, precipitation, financial freedom, eternal youth, the restoration of a limb – IT CAN BE DONE - but the 'stick-to-itiveness,' which is an important part of my ray and the qualification of the energy with my life, is required to produce these.

"The greatest obstacles encountered to successful precipitation are discouragement and doubt. I have seen men and women on the verge of the great financial mastery stop working on their project WITHIN AN HOUR of receiving their financial freedom! This also true in healing. I IMPLORE YOU – decide on some pattern and plan of manifestation and FOLLOW IT THROUGH! FOLOW IT THROUGH! FOLLOW IT THROUGH! CONCENTRATE upon your design until you have brought it into fulfillment.

"CONCENTRATION and CONSECRATION are almost one and the same, FOR WHATEVER YOU ARE GOING TO DO THAT WILL AMOUNT TO ANYTHING REQUIRES THE CONSCECRATION OF YOUR LIFE. It is the consecration of all your energies to the manifestation of something which will give you mastery over financial lack or mastery over appearances of physical distress is selfish, because the fully gathered momentum of your mastery becomes your gift to the consciousness of the race at large.

The energy which you magnetize, becomes yours to qualify and direct into the universe for good or ill. You qualify it by your thoughts, feelings, spoken words and acts, and that energy, moving in the irrevocable circle, sweeps out and then back to its creative center – YOU – for redemption. Each one of you took primal life and stamped upon it something of yourself, and that life, returning to you, is the karma of your various limitations and distresses. All such imperfections can be transmutes by the use of the VIOLET FIRE OF FREEDOM'S LOVE.

What is the CAUSE of FREEDOM? God is the CAUSE! The God-part of every man has within it the realization that FREEDOM and GODLINESS are one. The divine fiat of life is expansion, unfoldment, perfection – all of which qualities require FREEDOM in order to manifest. There is no such things as progress or evolution without FREEDOM. FREEDOM IS GOD IN ACTION. It is the divine plan that there shall be FREEDOM to all life – mankind, elementals, and angels.

"I tell you frankly, if you are going to succeed, YOU MUST BE POSITIVE, DETERMINED AND CONFIDENT within yourself. "The greatest opportunity in the world is to USE THIS FLAME OF FREEDOM, and to stand UNMOVED, CENTERED AND POISED WITHIN YOUR OWN GOD FLAME!

"Do not limit the powers of your "I AM" Presence, beloved ones. Become acquainted with that glorious Presence, because of its omnipotent power and its willingness to act to and through you, at all times. Personally, you could not possibly attempt to rehabilitate the entire human race – the three-and-one-billion who are in embodiment, besides those billions awaiting physical embodiment, BUT YOUR 'I AM' PRESENCE CAN!

"Your Presence and mine are not limited in any way! Your Presence is ALL KNOWING and IS CAPABLE OR DIRECTING INSTANTLY, FROM ITSELF, A BILLION RAYS OF TRANSCENDENT, BLAZING LIGHT INTO WHATEVER CONDITION PLACE OR PERSON REQUIRES ASSISTANCE.

"We are at the beginning of a New Age in which, through the courtesy and kindness of life, I am the Chohan and I will assist you in the religious service which will be manifested in the worship of the next two-thousand-year period. This is the activity of the VIOLET RAY, the activity of Ordered Service and Ritual, the activity where mankind, angels and elementals will again be drawn together in conscious cooperation, and will, hand in hand, walk together along the path of evolution, where they will serve together and build together, the Kingdom of Heaven on Earth. They will worship together in ceremonials such as you cannot yet conceive.

"Let that Violet Fire blaze up, through and around your physical body, you etheric, mental and emotional bodies, especially through your brain structure and feeling world, commanding it to transmute the hard and unforgiving feelings. These 'hard' feelings are the causes and cores of most of your distresses. Let them be replaces by grateful, joyous, receptive feelings, which open your world to the goodness of God and make you a mighty magnet to draw to you all the good that God wants you to have."

It is what a man is thinking, feeling and saying that creates around him an aura which rises as harmony, peace and healing. So on behalf of music, I want your souls to sing as you move about in the most mundane activities of daily living. In the light, there is no high or low position, there is only the eternal NOW, and the song of the soul that fills the aura and atmosphere where a truly devoted chela lives, is the greatest gift that can be given.

Harmony and music are wound into the activities of permanent healing – healing of every distress, moral, mental, emotional, etheric and physical.

LOVING LIFE FREE is the greatest service that there is in this universe.

FREEDOM – freedom from illness, limitation and distress. And where shall you find that freedom? FROM WITHIN YOUR OWN LIFE!

"In the beginning of your individualization, God created your divine, self-consciousness intelligence, your own individualized "I AM," a White Fire Being, from the Universal First Cause, with the capacity to draw forth from every life every God-gift you might require, to be able to manifest perfection. Within the flame in your heart is anything and everything that you require! I urge you to DEVELOP YOUR LIFE and the qualities which are within it. From that same primal life and light, we created the planet upon which your presently abide, as well as all the planets of this system.

"Call forth what you wish from the heart of that life which flows from the Universal, and if you wish to release into outer manifestation from within your own life whatever powers, qualities, gifts and activities are required to perfect your own world and that of your fellowman. Wherever there is a lifestream who sincerely desires FREEDOM, and in constant RHYTHM, invokes and commands it, there shall I be to give that one assistance, until that FREEDOM is physically manifest."

"In your individual application, if you will observe a RHYTHM, and give your individual calls AT THE SAME HOUR EACH DAY, you will draw a much more concentrated power."

CHANGE YOUR
SITUATION

CHAPTER 8

*"Always turn a negative situation
into a positive situation."*
- Michael Jordan -

WORDS FROM ASCENDED MASTER JESUS

(Extracted from 21 Essential Lessons)

"Beloved children of God, I come to bring to you my consciousness of victorious accomplishment. That which I have done and which I manifested through a flesh form similar to the one you presently wear, was not miraculous! It was something which is similarly ordained for every lifestream upon this planet. My endeavor to bring that manifestation of Christ fulfillment before the eyes of men, was merely to PROVIDE AN EXAMPLE by which every man, woman and child might be stirred to make effort toward a like development.

"One of the greatest mistakes, which has 'bogged down' the activity of the Christian Dispensation, is the placing of Godhood upon myself ALONE, and denying it to my fellowman. Christhood IS POSSIBLE FOR OTHERS, besides my humble self. Before I was born into my final embodiment, there were many lifestreams who had achieved the state of Christhood, full mastery and God-control, having sublimated the flesh form – knowing the victory of the ascension. However, for the Christian Dispensation, it was my great opportunity to manifest the resurrection, which is done so easily every spring by the nature kingdom. I was to come and bring the Divine Presence into the very substance of Earth, developing it into a God-man, made in the image and likeness of the Father who, in the first place, created me, and who also created you, in like manner.

"For every divine creation, whether it be angel, deva, seraphim, or human being, there is a divine pattern of perfection for that creation. In the case of the human being, it is called the 'individualized I AM Presence!' This divine pattern of perfection is fashioned out of living light, and within its heart is placed the Immortal Threefold Flame of Life. Within that flame is intelligence and consciousness.

"The SECOND COMING OF THE CHRIST means the awakening of many men and woman, who will externalize the glory of their divine pattern and plan through their outer selves. This was my message – it was my mission! It was the reason for coming into being, the reason for every experience of the Earth-life, even to allowing men to mutilate my flesh form. I allowed this, to prove that the immortality and divinity of the Godhead could be manifest through one of the sons of men!

"Are you less than a flowering bulb or a seed that produces after its kind? Are you less than a blade of grass, less than the embryo chicken, which bursts from the egg, following the pattern of its parents? Ah, no! YOU ARE FAR GREATER! You have one thing which is not the gift of the nature kingdom – FREE WILL! Through the use of that gift of free will, you have chosen to NOT let the God who created you (and who is living within your heart) to expand into its full perfection."

"I say to your consciousness, your minds, and your bodies, in the name of the one mighty god, PEACE UNTO YOU! PEACE BE UNTO YOUR STRIVING CONSCIOUSNESS, YOUR RESTLESS MINDS, AND YOUR WEARY BODIES – THE PEACE OF GOD THAT DOES SURPASS THE UNDERSTANDING OF THE OUTER MIND! Let it enter NOW into every cell and fiber of your being and relax in the knowledge that you are IMMERSED IN THE PRESENCE OF THE ALMIGHT. You live, move, and truly have your being within the living, breathing intelligent body of the universal God, and no matter how far you may stray in thought, you can never leave the safety of his bosom. It but requires of you the awakening to your presence within that safe, secure and loving heart!

"YOU ARE IN TRAINING TO BECOME MASTERS! FEEDOME COMES WHEN YOU ARE MASTER OF CIRCUMSTANCES CONSCIOUSLY AND CAN REGULATE ANY SET OF CIRCUMSTANCES BY THE FLAME WITHIN YOUR HEART. THERE IS NO OTHER PERMANENT FREEDOME! In the

schoolroom of life, it would be easier to have an individual who had passed successfully through your course, work your problems for you, but the wise man learns the principle himself, lest the man on whom he relies to solve his problems, should not be there when his great opportunity comes.

The beloved Ascended Masters Jesus, in recalling his mission 2000 years ago, said to the students:

"My ministry was one of action. Every day before leaving my home, great numbers of people would gather to receive relief from all manner of discomfort and disease of mind and body. Very few came to learn the technique which enabled me to alleviate their distress. I NEVER, NEVER went forth to serve UNTIL I HAD FIRST ANCHORED MY CONSCIOUSNESS in the feeling and presence of God. Only when I had contemplated God and firmly established my unshakable faith, that indestructible fortress of God's power and Omni-presence, would I endeavor to convey that consciousness of God's goodness through words and worked to my fellowman."

FINAL NOTE

I would lastly like to share that I am by no means a perfect human being. No one is. We all have all past and present flaws or experiences in which we will always need to work on and improve. I firmly believe that everyone on this planet has something that they need to work on to obtain understanding and peace in order to live a purposeful life. If we hold hatred in our hearts of any kind, we are not fulfilling all the joys that life has to offer us. We are actually delaying positive progress and stopping good things from happening to us.

I've been through hell and back, while still taking a moment to forgive and let the universe handle the rest. The saying is very true, we may forgive, but we will never forget. It's important not to forget the bad things that happen because they shape us into who we are meant to be. We may not always understand what the higher powers are doing up there, however, we can open up our minds and release the negative energies that try to break us down.

Letting go of hurt, bitterness, sadness, grief, pain, dishonesty, and negativity will ease away future discrepancies that try to overcome, by us changing the outcome. If we treat other good, we receive good things in return. The same results surface if we treat others badly. I am always working on implementing what the world needs more of, by ensuring that I can walk in love, speak love, and continuously; wholeheartedly - Just Be Love!

CULTIVATE

EXPLORE

OWN

Over the last several years, I have come into connection with a beautiful world, career, and life. Most of all, I love people. No matter what their background or culture.

I've learned that it is vital to keep learning about the world that we live in. Don't judge or be envious. Don't hate or ridicule. Don't lie or be deceitful. Just be love and the universe will unfold in ways you've never imaged. Doors will open that you may feel have been closed. And light will shine upon you in your darkest hours.

Simply put: Life is beautiful. We all just have to open our hearts to mankind, and that one step alone will make our world a little more perfect.

I would love for you to follow me on my social networks, as I travel the world.

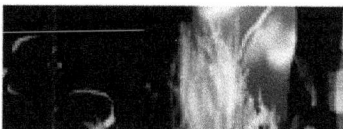

PARTICIPATE

CREATE

SATISFY

Exploring. Learning. Giving. And Loving.

Stay connected with my international endeavors by visiting my social platforms:

www.TheTreniaTodayShow.TV
www.TreniaToday.com

Follow me on Twitter: *@TreniaToday*

#TreniaToday
#TheTreniaTodayShow

www.ingramcontent.com/pod-product-compliance
Lightning Source LLC
Chambersburg PA
CBHW061738020426
42331CB00006B/1283